DISSECTING THE *ACT*®*2.0

ACT TEST PREPARATION ADVICE OF A PERFECT SCORER
ACT TEST PREP WITH REAL ACT QUESTIONS

By

Rajiv Raju

and

Silpa Raju

Platypus Global Media

Published in the United States of America by:

Platypus Global Media

Registered with the U.S. ISBN agency

Contact Publisher at: ***pgmdirect@gmail.com***

Distribution worldwide by **Ingram Book Company**

www.ingrambook.com

Available from major wholesalers in U.S., U.K. and E.U.

Printed at multiple locations worldwide.

This Second Edition Published September 2009 and contains 80%
new material to reflect the new official practice test (**Form 0964E**)
released by the *ACT.*

ISBN-13: 978-0-9842212-1-9

ISBN-10: 0-9842212-1-2

CONTENTS

INTRODUCTION   1

SUGGESTED ACT PREP PLAN   5

ACT ENGLISH CONCEPTS   7

ACT ENGLISH EXPLANATIONS   25

ACT MATHEMATICS CONCEPTS   49

ACT MATHEMATICS EXPLANATIONS   73

ACT READING STRATEGY   101

ACT READING EXPLANATIONS   107

ACT SCIENCE REASONING STRATEGY   123

ACT SCIENCE EXPLANATIONS   127

ACT ESSAY (WRITING) STRATEGY   143

Notes

PREFACE

The authors created this book to provide an inexpensive and concise resource to help students improve their ACT score. Most high school students are very busy and they can not devote too much time to ACT test preparation. Whatever time they spend for preparation should be spent using resources that are relevant to the real test, not on books that contain irrelevant and inaccurate representations of the test. The focus of this book is entirely on the *real* test. While the ACT expects you have some factual knowledge of mathematical concepts, grammar concepts and punctuation rules, there is a great deal of emphasis on thinking skills. In fact the ACT Reading and Science Reasoning sections do not require any specific knowledge. Even the English section has a large number of rhetorical skills questions that can not be answered with knowledge of grammar rules alone. The Mathematics section also has many questions which require the application of concepts in novel ways. These questions test higher order thinking skills that can not be easily summarized. The only way to improve these skills in the short run is to practice and analyze real test questions. **This book provides specific information about how to get free access to three full real ACT tests, with a total of 645 real test questions.** The authors provide a detailed analysis of one of these tests. In addition, the authors have identified and listed the most essential factual knowledge that is necessary for success on the ACT test. The reader should find this work to be unlike anything else on the market.

Rajiv Raju and Silpa Raju
South Barrington, IL
September 2009

AUTHORS

Rajiv Raju is a student at Barrington High School (IL) at the time of publication. He wrote the Mathematics, Science and Reading sections of this book. He wrote this book to create an inexpensive resource to prepare for the ACT. Using strategies summarized in this book, he scored a perfect 36 on the ACT. In his free time, Rajiv likes to, hang out with friends and play Indian classical violin. He also likes to play the electric guitar and enjoys listening to his large collection of music.

Silpa Raju is also a student at Barrington High School (IL) at the time of publication. She wrote the English and Writing sections of this book. She took the ACT in the 9th grade to qualify for summer programs and scored a 35 on the English component of the ACT. In her spare time, Silpa enjoys singing opera music, spending time with friends and reading.

INTRODUCTION

Although this second edition has 80% new content, the introductory comments are similar to the first edition. This edition has been updated for the new official free practice test **Form 0964E** and also includes new tips and strategies for all sections of the ACT.

Why another ACT test prep book?

There is no shortage of ACT test preparation books on the market. Almost all of these books, with the exception of the book from the test makers, have one very serious shortcoming: they attempt to create ACT type test questions. More often than not, these questions are not accurate representations of the real exam. Many of these books have irrelevant and inaccurate material and often have questions that do not have the correct level of difficulty. Making real ACT questions requires enormous resources that only the test makers have. This book makes no attempt to make up simulated questions, but instead focuses on an analysis of real ACT questions for one complete real ACT examination- dissecting the test, in other words. This complete real ACT test is available free of charge from the test maker. This analysis is performed by authors who have actually taken the ACT and have obtained high scores. In addition, the analysis of the test is from a student's perspective rather than from a teacher's or a test maker's perspectives. This unique perspective enables the authors to share insights not found in any other books. Using this book will give the reader a deep and accurate understanding of the skills and knowledge necessary for success on the real ACT test. This is the first step in maximizing one's score.

In addition to performing a detailed analysis of the official practice test, the authors have also evaluated other real ACT tests that are publically available and have identified the most important knowledge and thinking skills that are tested frequently on the ACT. These concepts are summarized for efficient review. Knowing the essential concepts is only the beginning; doing well on the ACT requires you to apply these concepts in ways that are often quite different from what is expected in school. In our opinion, the most effective preparation should include practice and analysis of real ACT questions. The next chapter includes a complete and detailed ACT test preparation plan that goes beyond this book and provides specific information about how to obtain three free real ACT tests.

Where do I get the real ACT questions?

The ACT provides a free booklet called <u>Preparing for the ACT</u>. It can be obtained for free at most high schools and directly from the ACT. The PDF file of this booklet can also be downloaded free from the ACT website at:

http://www.act.org/aap/pdf/preparing.pdf

This book assumes that you have the booklet, <u>Preparing for the ACT</u>, released for the academic year 2009/2010. This booklet has the free test **Form 0964E**. We expect this booklet to be unchanged for 2010/2011 and 2011/2012 academic years, since in the past the ACT has changed questions in the booklet every three years. If you happen to get this book when the booklet with the current set of questions is no longer available from the ACT, send a message to the email address below for the most current link to the PDF file of the booklet needed to use this book at:

dissectingact@yahoo.com

What about the book from the makers of the ACT?

<u>The Real ACT Prep Guide</u> which is made by the makers of the ACT is an excellent book and is highly recommended. This book has real ACT questions with explanations. Unfortunately it appears that the test makers do not want to give up too much specific information about what one is expected to know. For example, in the math content list on page 50 and 51 of the book, you will see a very general list of topics that is not very helpful. Under the trigonometry category "trigonometric identities" is listed. Are we expected to know all of the identities in the trigonometry book? <u>The Real ACT Prep Guide</u> does not explicitly tell you which specific formulas you must know. The authors of <u>Dissecting the ACT</u> have analyzed real ACT tests and

identified what formulas and concepts the test makers expect you to know. The reader should find our book a useful complement to The Real ACT Prep Guide.

Organization of this book.

For each of the four major sections of the ACT, there is an introductory section which lists important content and skills needed for the section. There is also a strategy guide for the optional ACT Writing test, or essay. To illustrate how the concepts are tested, for some of the sections references will be made to real questions from the booklet, Preparing for the ACT. This is followed by an analysis of every question in the sample test. Some may feel that the content identified in this book is not comprehensive enough, but the objective of this book is not to be comprehensive- rather, it is to identify the concepts that are tested very frequently and therefore considered essential. The conventional wisdom is that a good high school education is the only comprehensive preparation for the ACT. While this may be true, the ACT only covers a small subset of what you learn in school. The most effective way to improve ones score is to understand what this subset of knowledge is and to understand how it is tested on the real ACT. The objective of the book is to identify the most frequently tested concepts and explain how they are tested by analyzing real questions.

Comparison with the SAT

Those who have prepared for the SAT should be aware of some important differences between the two tests. When dealing with the SAT there are debates about when to guess and when to leave an answer choice blank. On the ACT there is no debate about filling in answer choices. There is no guessing penalty on the ACT whatsoever. You should always fill in an answer bubble even if you did not read the question. The SAT usually has five answer choices, but most of the ACT only has four answer choices. This gives random guessing even more of an advantage. The Math section of ACT is the only section that has 5 answer choices. If you are running out of time and can not finish a section, make every effort to fill in an answer for each question.

Some parts of the SAT have easy questions at the beginning of the section and more difficult questions towards the end of section. There is no such order on the ACT. Never waste time on difficult questions. Guess and move on. If you dwell on difficult questions, you may not have time to attempt easy questions that may appear later on the test. This can hurt your score, and it is a shame to lose points on questions that you can otherwise answer if you get to them.

The ACT gives you significantly less time per question than the SAT. Correct pacing during the exam is *extremely* critical on the ACT. The English section has perhaps the most brutal time constraints, giving you only about 36 seconds per question on average! The math allots you a minute per question, making it the most generous section on the test. Both the science and reading give you slightly less than a minute to do each question. Most students who take the test seem to think that the time constraints are the biggest obstacle for them to overcome.

Although SAT is called the "Reasoning Test", the ACT also tests reasoning skills. In fact the "Science Reasoning" section on the ACT is almost entirely a reasoning test. The ACT English section tests all of the skills tested in the SAT writing multiple choice section, but also tests punctuation rules which do not show up on the SAT. The ACT math includes a few questions on more advanced topics, such as trigonometry. There is also the sporadic logical reasoning question, which can be answered with careful inference.

SUGGESTED ACT PREP PLAN

Save time and money- only use real tests!

We feel that effective ACT preparation should not require wealthy parents who are willing to pay hundreds, and in some cases thousands, of dollars for a prep class. We wrote this book to create an inexpensive resource that will let any person improve their score at least as much as a student in an expensive prep class can, if not more.

Get the free booklet Preparing for the ACT from your school or the ACT organization. You can also download it free form this link:

http://www.act.org/aap/pdf/preparing.pdf

Read the introductory portions of our book Dissecting the ACT 2.0 and start doing the questions without any time limits. After doing each question, immediately read the explanation in our book that corresponds to that question. **Read the explanation even if you get the right answer**, since the explanations may give you insights that could help you with other questions. The objective is to really understand how the ACT tests your skills and how you can adapt your thinking to do well on the test. After going through all the questions in this booklet, Dissecting the ACT 2.0, you should have a very good idea of what it takes to get a good score. After doing this, go to this link:

http://www.actstudent.org/sampletest/index.html

There is another full free official test from the ACT at this link, and it even has explanations. While you do these questions pay attention to how long it takes to do the questions and see if you can develop your own strategies to increase your speed and accuracy. Identify any weak areas and go back and study the introductory content of our book. Following this, you can take a third free real ACT practice test under timed conditions. This test is available as a free download from the internet archive at this link:

http://web.archive.org/web/20050305184755/www.actstudent.org/pdf/preparing.pdf

Be patient with this link, since it can be very slow. We will also have this link in the Amazon authors' blog so that you can get the free test easily.

You should now be ready to give the real ACT a try, but do not send the score to any colleges until you get the score that you are happy with. You can take the ACT multiple times and send the colleges your best score, although a few colleges require you to send all the scores. **If you are planning to apply to any of the colleges that require all the scores, then you should only take the test with adequate preparation.** The night before the test go over all the mistakes that you have made on the three real practice tests that you took so far.

If you are not happy with the score you get on your first try, get the book The Real ACT Prep Guide published by the test makers. This book has three more real ACT tests with explanations. You can buy this book new for about $16 on Amazon.com or get a used version of this book via Amazon.com for as little as $5. After taking the three tests in Real ACT Prep Guide, sign up for the test again and see how you do.

If you are still not happy with your score and feel that you need more practice with real tests, the ACT has an Online Course for $20. We have not taken this course, but we do know that includes two full real practice tests. We do not know how useful the rest of the course is, but the two official practice tests should be useful. After taking the two practice tests, sign up for the real test again. By now you have taken a total of 10 real ACT tests (8 at home and 2 for real) and you should be ready to ace the test. You have spent less than $50 on test prep, and should be at least as well prepared as those who have taken expensive courses.

ACT ENGLISH CONCEPTS
By **Silpa Raju**

Key English Strategies:

-Punctuation questions can be answered using punctuation rules.

-Rhetorical skills questions are more complex and require you to think about the passage.

- Use grammar rules when possible, but go with your intuition when in doubt.

-Do not get too hung up on complex grammar rules. Your time is better spent practicing on real ACT questions so that your brain gets a feel for correct answers.

The ACT English test requires much less grammar knowledge than what you may have learned in school. In fact, only a small subset of grammar concepts is repeatedly tested. The ACT never tests any grammar terminology. Since the ACT is locked into a multiple choice format, you are only required to recognize and correct poor use of language. However, in order to discuss the concepts that are tested on the ACT, it is necessary to introduce a limited amount of grammar terminology. The concepts described below are only intended for use on the ACT and may not be considered correct by your English teacher. The concepts will make much more sense when you see them used in real questions.

TERMINOLOGY

Noun- a person, place, thing or concept
Examples: John, Chicago, teacher, house

Pronouns- a subset of nouns that are used as substitute for another noun

Examples: I, you, he, she, it, we, they, me, you, him, her, us, them, one, which, that

Subject- a noun that does the action

Object- a noun that receives the action

Avery kicked the ball.

In this sentence above, Avery is the subject because she is the one kicking the ball, and the object is the ball, because the ball is being kicked.

Adjective- a word that modifies a noun

Example: Fast car; Fast modifies car.

Verb- an action word

Examples: sing, fall, scream

Adverb-modifies a verb, adjective or adverb

Adverbs can be identified most of the time by their ending: words ending in -ly are often adverbs.

Examples: kindly, gently, angrily

Article- a word that modifies or limits a noun

Examples: a, an, the

Phrase- a group of words that does not have both a noun and a verb at once and acts as a single part of speech.

Preposition – describes relative positions of ideas.

Avni screamed as a spider scurried over her toe.

The preposition is "over." The prepositional phrase is "over her toe".

Clause-a group of words that have both a noun and verb

Independent clause- Has a complete thought and can stand alone as a sentence

Dependent clause- Has noun and verb, but can not stand alone as a sentence

STRUCTURE AND GRAMMAR

A large portion of the ACT English section tests skills in sentence arrangement and parallelism. Let's move through all the structural errors tested on the ACT.

Errors in Sentence Structure
The Comma Splice

Two independent clauses can not be joined with only a comma, as in the following sentence:

He was too lazy to take down last year's calendar, it is still sitting there.

This sentence has a comma splice, but there are many ways to fix it.

We can add a period and make two sentences, like so:

He was too lazy to take down last year's calendar. It is still sitting there.

We can also add a conjunction after the comma.

He was too lazy to take down last year's calendar, so it is still sitting there.

We can even add a semicolon:

He was too lazy to take down last year's calendar; it is still sitting there.

Any of these fixes might show up as options in an ACT English test question.

The Run-On Sentence

A run-on sentence happens when two independent clauses are put together without punctuation. This is a run-on:

Gabrielle wanted to go to the party she was grounded.

The run on sentence can be fixed with punctuation just like the comma splice, and can also be fixed with a conjunction.

Gabrielle wanted to go to the party, but she was grounded.

Sentence Fragments

Fragments are just dependent clauses waiting to be completed. These do not form a complete thought, and they can not stand alone as a proper sentence. The following is a fragment:

When Jake was waking up.

To fix a fragment to make a grammatically correct sentence, you'll need to do one of the following:

Add an independent clause with a comma and a dependent clause:

When Jake was waking up, he realized he was late for work.

Take away the word that makes this a dependent clause (when):

Jake was waking up.

Parallelism and Agreement

Many ACT questions test parallelism/agreement in the form of tenses, plurality, etc.

Pronoun-Noun Plurality Issue

Every person who suffered through the period of the Black Plague certainly was thankful for their life.

In the above sentence, "every" is a singular word; therefore, the word "their" must also be singular.

Every person who suffered through the period of the Black Plague certainly was thankful for his or her life.

"His or her" is singular and now matches the plurality of "every".

Pronoun Usage: Subject or Object Pronoun?

In a sentence, you use certain pronouns to describe a subject and certain pronouns to describe an object.

Here are a few examples:

Subject Pronouns: he, she, it, they
Object pronouns: him, her, me, whom

Take a look at this sentence:

Me took a nap yesterday.

Since "me" is the subject, you should use a subject pronoun.

I took a nap yesterday.

Who/Whom

Probably one of the most baffling concepts for many test takers is the usage of who/whom. It's actually simpler than you think. The same rules about pronoun usage can be applied to the usage of who/whom. Try thinking of it in terms of she/her.

Who=she

Whom=her

(Who/whom) read the novel?

Her didn't read the novel, she did, so you would say who.

For (who/whom) should I buy a bouquet of flowers?

You would buy a bouquet for her, not for she, so you would say whom

Parallelism with Nouns and Verbs

When you see a series of nouns or verbs, be sure that they're all in the same tense or structure.

Noun parallelism

Though Adam was quite the intelligent student, he repelled a stereotypically nerdy persona with his sense of style, his street smarts, and his loving of life beyond video games.

This might not sound incorrect, but if you look closely, there is a lack of parallel structure in the third listed phrase. "his loving" should be "his love" because "his love" would match the structure of "his sense" and "his street smarts"

Verb Parallelism

Kelsey had to do three things on Friday: she needed to cook for her family, to go to an aerobics class, and picking up cash from the bank.

The same tense issue is present in this list of verbs. The first two verbs are in their infinitive form, ("to cook" and "to go") while the last verb is not. "Picking" should be "to pick" to make it a parallel tense.

Incorrect Placement of Modifying Phrase

A modifier phrase modifies another part of the sentence. The modifying phrase must be near the subject it is modifying to avoid confusion.

While reading a withered copy of Romeo and Juliet, fatigue came over Xiao.

This sentence reads like fatigue was reading Romeo and Juliet. Be sure to rearrange the sentence so it reads properly.

While reading a withered copy of Romeo and Juliet, Xiao was over come by fatigue.

While riding his bike, $150 dollars was found by Alex.

In the second incorrect example, its structure implies that the $150 was riding the bike. Of course, we know that Alex was the one who was riding the bike and stumbled upon the $150.

While riding his bike, Alex found $150 dollars.

Agreement- Subject/Verb

A subject should agree with the verb in a sentence in terms of plurality.

Take a look at this incorrect example:

The part Liz hated most in the book were at the end.

In this sentence, the subject is "the part" and the verb is "were". Since the subject is singular, the verb must also be singular.

The part Liz hated the most in the book was at the end.

Now the subject and verb agree in plurality.

When pronouns are functioning as subjects, don't be fooled by their plurality.

Each of the chapters in the book have a title.

The subject is ONE *chapter* because the sentence says "each of the chapters" which is singular. Therefore, the verb "have" must also be singular.

Each of the chapters in the book has a title.

Now the verb "has" is singular and shares the same plurality with "each".

Adjectives vs. Adverbs

Recall the difference between adverbs and adjectives from the terminology section. Adjectives only modify nouns, while adverbs describe other parts of speech.

Emily opened the door briefly.

This sentence is correct because the adverb "briefly" is describing "opened". Now look at this incorrect sentence:

Avni's boyfriend, Chris, is kindly.

This sentence is incorrect because the adverb "kindly" should actually be an adjective because it's referring to the noun Chris.

Avni's boyfriend, Chris, is kind.

The sentence is now correct because "kind" is an adjective.

PUNCTUATION

Commas

The ACT heavily tests your knowledge of comma placement. Let's review where to put them.

Commas are used to:

Separate more than two items in a list-

Farah's dog ran under the table, through the kitchen, and into a wall.

Separating parts of sentences-

Think independent and dependent clauses, as well as phrases.

Separating two independent clauses- When a sentence contains two independent clauses, they are often joined by a conjunction, if not a semicolon or other means of connection. Placing a comma before the conjunction is proper.

Incorrect: *Austin was out for a run when he saw a ring on the path so he picked it up and gave it to his girlfriend.*

Correct: *Austin was out for a run when he saw a ring on the path, so he picked it up and gave it to his girlfriend.*

Commas are used to separate a modifier phrase from the thing that is being modified.

Filled with excitement, Monica ripped open her ACT results, tearing the report in the process.

In the above sentence, a comma separates the modifying phrase "filled with excitement" from the subject being modified, Monica.

Commas are also used to separate parenthetical expressions.

Miguel, the star of the track team, won at state.

In this example "the star of the track team" is the parenthetical phrase since it can be removed and the sentence still makes sense. If removing a phrase significantly changes the meaning of a sentence, then it is not a parenthetical phrase and should not be separated with commas.

Semicolons

The semicolon is used to separate two independent clauses that are closely related. If you see the semicolon used anywhere else on the ACT, it is being misused.

Silpa was a big spender; she became more frugal when her parents cut off her allowance.

In this sentence, both halves are independent clauses that can stand alone. This is an appropriate use of the semicolon.

Colons

Colons are used to introduce a list at the end of an independent clause and can only be used at the end of an independent clause. The list may contain one or many items.

Neha counted up the new items she bought while shopping yesterday: two shirts, a pair of jeans, and perfume.

Apostrophes

Apostrophes can be used to indicate missing letters in a word. For example, you can use an apostrophe to shorten "I am" to "I'm". Such contractions must be memorized, but fortunately we use most of them in everyday talk. Apostrophes are also used to indicate possession.

Stuart's new car is very fast.

If possession applies to a plural noun ending in "s" then the apostrophe comes after the "s."

The meeting is in the students' lounge.

Wrong answer choices on the ACT often use superfluous apostrophes. The object being possessed must follow the word that has the apostrophe. If this is not the case then an apostrophe is not needed.

Rules are different for "its" and "it's".

The word "it's" means "it is."

The word "its' " is always incorrect. If you see "its' " with the apostrophe after the "s" on the ACT, it is an incorrect choice.

The word "its" indicates possession. There is no apostrophe here.

Dashes

Use dashes like you would use parentheses. Use two dashes unless the parenthetical expression comes at the end of a sentence.

Nayan took his vitamin pill- just like he does everyday- right after dinner.

Or

Nayan took his vitamin pill- he always takes them after dinner.

RHETORICAL SKILLS

A large portion of the English test is made of rhetorical skills questions. Rhetorical skills questions test ideas that can't be memorized, but require a bit of thinking. They often require some basic writing skill. Here we'll go over some of the types of rhetorical skills questions present on the ACT English test. A good rule of thumb is to pick options that are most concise while still getting the point across. In the end, you want to pick options that fit the tone of the essay best- this is one of the hardest issues on the English test.

Ordering Sentences/Paragraphs

The ACT will on occasion ask you to pick the best order for sentences or paragraphs. The best way to do this is to think about which parts flow best in what order. This is where writer's sense comes in. What is the most logical order for sentences or paragraphs to go in? Do they keep a consistent flow of thought with smooth transitions? Arrange the sentences or paragraphs in an order you think flows easily.

Strategy

The ACT will ask you to edit the passage to make it better. To help you more accurately answer these questions, identify the point of the passage itself and also the audience it serves. Think about what you are putting in/cutting out in terms of the purpose of the passage and the readers.

Redundancy

The ACT tests redundancy in sentences. If you see a sentence using two synonyms right next to each other, you can pretty much assume that you need to axe one of them.

My friend played online Internet games daily in the year 1996.

In this sentence, it is implied that online games are on the Internet, and that 1996 is a year.

My friend played online games daily in 1996.

This sentence eliminates the unnecessary wording.

Unclear Pronoun Reference

When you have a sentence with two nouns and you use a pronoun, it may be unclear as to which noun you are referring to.

Tommy and Billy are good friends, but he is nicer.

In this sentence, it is not clear who "he" is talking about. Make it clear by removing the pronoun altogether and inserting a noun.

Tommy and Billy are good friends, but Billy is nicer.

Transitions

Some questions will ask you to choose the best transition to complete a sentence. You'll need to know the meanings of the transitions, but most of them are used in everyday speech so it shouldn't be a problem. Here's an example:

LaTonya missed home while she was at college, (but/because) she also enjoyed dorm life.

When picking a transition, think about what it means. "But" is introducing two viewpoints or ideas, while "because" is cause and effect. Look for key words in the sentence that hint at what is going on. In the sentence above, "also" is introducing another perspective. "But" is a transition that means two different ideas or viewpoints. "Because" is a transition that is used for cause and effect. Since "also" is showing a different idea and not the result of something, we can use the transition "but".

OTHER TIDBITS

Idiom errors

One error that can't really be taught is an idiom error. To solve such questions on the ACT, all you can do is acquaint yourself with the English language through exposure. Idiom error questions generally test whether you know to use the right preposition or not. Here's an incorrect example:

Oscar went of the car.

"Of" is certainly not the right preposition to use here.

Oscar went to the car.

This sentence employs the proper use of a preposition.

No Change/Omit

The ACT gives you a couple of repeated options. It is important to not neglect these choices, like many test takers do.

-No change:
        The "no change" option is present on most questions in the writing test. Don't make up an error that's not there- for about a fourth of the questions, there is nothing wrong at all.

-Omit the underlined portion:

The "omit the underlined portion" option is often seen in rhetorical skills questions. Sometimes, an extra sentence or phrase isn't necessary, and the test writers want you to just get rid of unnecessary wording, hence this option- in fact, when this answer is available, it's correct more than 50% of the time. If you feel a passage could do without a sentence, cutting it out isn't a bad idea.

Notes

ACT ENGLISH TEST EXPLANATIONS
By **Silpa Raju**

Please refer to the questions in the English component of the practice test (**Form 0964E**) in official ACT booklet, Preparing for the ACT .

1.   This question is testing parallel structure. Look at the sentence- "Unbricking a kiln after a firing is like a person uncovering buried treasure." For the sentence to have parallel structure, the verb "unbricking" should be compared to another verb, not a noun Unbricking a kiln is not like the actual person, it is like uncovering buried treasure. The word "person" creates confusion and is portraying the wrong idea. Choice A, or no change, is incorrect because of this. Answer B is also wrong because using the word "someone" creates the same error as in choice A. Choice C is incorrect for the same reason. Replacing "a person" with "a potter" does not fix the error. The correct answer is D because by cutting "a person" out of the sentence, you get "unbricking a kiln after a firing is like uncovering buried treasure". The sentence employs parallel structure because it is comparing "unbricking" to "uncovering", both of which are verbs.

2.   This is a rhetorical skills question. The question asks you to pick the choice that implies a slow, careful pace and excitement. Choice F, "takes bricks away", doesn't imply any sort of pace or caution, it's just a generalized statement that could be slow or fast. It's too dry to communicate emotion, either. Choice G, "removes bricks by hand", shows caution but doesn't show any emotion. Choice J only displays emotion (anticipation) but says "removes bricks", which doesn't tell us anything about caution or the pace at which the person is removing bricks. Answer H is the correct answer because it tells you that the person carefully removed bricks by hand, and also subtly shows the anticipation as the view of the products in the kiln becomes larger as each brick is taken away. The way the answer says "removes one brick at a time", it gives a sense of building excitement as each brick is taken away. If you look at the sentence as a whole, it says in the second half "to create an opening into the oven, an expanding view of gleaming shapes rewards the artist for months of

hard work". Taking away one brick at a time goes along with "an expanding view" as well.

3.   This question also tests parallelism, this time in verb tenses and plurality. The answer to the question should match the tense of "takes", which is present tense. Choice B is incorrect because it uses the present progressive tense (-ing verbs, in this case rewarding), not present tense. Answer C is also incorrect because "reward" is plural and "view" is singular. Notice how "reward" corresponds to "view" and not to "shapes". Answer D is wrong because using the phrase "as a reward for" would make the sentence a fragment. The correct answer is A because it agrees in both tense and plurality. The tense is present, and "rewards" is singular, like "view".

4.   This question tests idiom usage. It is difficult to learn idioms in any other way then seeing them in writing, so there is no reason why one works and another doesn't. Choice G is the correct answer because it uses proper idiomatic structure.

5.   This question is a good example of the ACT testing redundancy. All of the incorrect answers are actually grammatically correct, but it has already been mentioned that time has passed by the phrase "over many weeks" so it is unnecessary to add another phrase implying time passage. The correct answer is D because it eliminates redundancy by removing the phrase "as time goes by". This is implied in the passing of weeks, which makes it unnecessary.

6.   Sentence structure is being tested in this question. Recall the ways in which a sentence can be built with independent and dependent clauses, and transitions. Choice F is incorrect because by using the phrase "it is a brick structure", you are making the second half of the sentence an independent clause and since the first half is an independent clause and there is no transition, it makes the sentence a run-on. Answer G is incorrect for the same reason. Answer J is incorrect because, though it is grammatically correct, the brick itself isn't designed to bake pottery, the brick structure is, and by just using the word "brick" that isn't clear. The correct answer is H because it is grammatically correct- "a brick structure" makes the second half of the sentence a dependent clause, making the sentence arrangement independent clause followed by dependent clause.

7.   This is another rhetorical skills question. Answer A is wrong because the statement "and transforming glazes to glorious colors" is describing the kiln firing process, not the painting process or how time consuming it is. Answer C is wrong because it doesn't make sense- the portion the question asks about is telling you the function of the kiln, in this case that it transforms glazes to glorious colors, and answer C is saying that the statement doesn't focus on the function of the kiln when in fact it does. To verify that answer D is incorrect, you have to look at the level of detail thus far in the writing and make a decision about whether the amount of detail matches. Since the author has already talked in moderate detail about the unbricking of kilns and the function of a kiln, it is safe to say that adding another portion about the function of the kiln is an acceptable amount of detail in comparison to what has previously been said. Answer B is the correct answer because the author is talking about what a kiln does, and the statement is indeed relevant to the function of the kiln.

8.   Wordiness is being tested in this question. Recall that in many cases the shortest answer choice is the best, provided that it gets the point across. Choice G is incorrect because it is implied that she is stooping since the first half of the sentence talks about crouching. Choice H is incorrect for the same reason. J is wrong because Ellen isn't carefully stooping, she is carefully arranging and the way that phrase is arranged it makes it seem as if she is carefully stooping. The correct answer is F because it tells the reader she is carefully arranging, and since the reader already knows she's bending over to put things in the kiln it isn't included in the phrase. Coincidentally, the correct answer happens to be the most concise.

9.   Punctuation is being tested in this question. Choice A is incorrect because the two commas used to set off a phrase in a sentence should encompass the whole phrase "using twigs for kindling" and in A it only sets apart "using twigs", separating the thought "using twigs" and "for kindling". Answer C is wrong because a semi-colon is used to connect two independent clauses and the first part of the sentence is a dependent clause, so you can't put a semi-colon there. Answer D is also wrong for the same reason as A. The correct answer is B because it properly uses commas to set off an extra thought without breaking it apart like in A and D.

10.   Question 10 is a rhetorical skills question. In these questions you have to rely on your writing skill. Although all the choices do somewhat imply a strong fire, it comes to the point where you just have to choose the one that implies a strong fire but also sounds the best. Choice F is the best answer because without blatantly saying "the fire was strong" or "it produced a lot of heat" or "the fire was intense", you are saying it was strong with the use of the word "inferno".

11.   This question tests idiom usage. The question asks which phrase wouldn't be acceptable to replace "occasionally". To know which phrase is has proper idiom usage, you just have to have seen them in literature previously. The only option that has improper idiom usage is D- the "or" doesn't fit.

12.   This is yet another question testing idiom usage, in this case using the proper preposition. Choice G is an incorrect answer because ashes can shoot up the chimney. Answer H is an incorrect answer because ashes can go through the chimney, and choice J is a wrong answer because ashes can go out the chimney. The only preposition that doesn't make sense is in choice F, because thinking about it logically, ashes wouldn't shoot at the chimney. You would have to use some word that implied going through the chimney. Therefore, Choice F is the correct answer.

13.   Here's another rhetorical skills question. Keep in mind we're trying to maintain the same tone of the passage while saying that the temperature was hot. A is incorrect because "soars out of sight" is not suited to the tone of the essay. Answer B is incorrect for the same reason; because "beyond belief" does not fit the descriptive prose-type writing of this essay. Though "beyond belief" is descriptive, it is not the kind of specific descriptive the essay needs. D is incorrect because it says in a very complicated the same thing as C, especially with the mention of "increments". Obviously, temperature rises in "increments"- that is, degrees. It isn't necessary to use that complex of wording. C is the correct answer because it gives you a number to work with, and suits the tone of the essay with its more specific description (more specific than the other options, anyway).

14.   This is a misplaced modifier question. Look at the sentence: "Having died down, she bricks..." doesn't make sense. She didn't die down, the fire did. Knowing the error, we can choose the answer that refers to the fire and not Ellen. Choice F is incorrect for this reason. Answer G is wrong because it is a run-on and it says "finally it dies" in reference to Ellen instead of the fire. Answer H is wrong because Ellen doesn't brick the kiln "with a fire that dies", that just doesn't make sense. Choice J is correct because instead of referring to Ellen, it refers to the blaze by saying "once the blaze dies down". This is necessary to make it clear that Ellen is not the one dying down, and is the only choice that emphasizes so.

15.   This question tests preposition use. B is wrong because her labor is not from the fire's magic- it's just her own work that led to the results. C is incorrect because if you read it, it says "revealing the results of her labor, of which the fire is magic". That completely makes no sense whatsoever. Contextually, "of which the fire is magic" does not fit into the sentence. Answer D is incorrect because you're trying to speak of the effects of the fire's magic, and if you use that phrase it's like saying "revealing the results of her labor, and oh by the way, the fire is magic". You need to connect the idea of the fire's magic to the result, and answer D fails to do so. Choice A is the best answer because it is both grammatically correct and it links the magic of the fire, and the labor of Ellen, to the end result of the products from the Kiln.

16.   Redundancy is being tested in this question. F is wrong because it is implied that a business trip is connected to work, so it is unnecessary to use both phrases, you only need one. Answer G is incorrect because a business trip clearly has something to do with his job, otherwise it wouldn't be a business trip. Using both phrases would be repetitive. H is incorrect because the fact that he's going to another city is not pertinent to the story because we already know that she'll have to stay with someone else, so it's not important to know where he is going, only that he won't be staying with her. The best choice is J, or to delete the whole portion, which eliminates the redundancy issues.

17.   This question tests idiom usage. It asks you to pick the choice which wouldn't be an acceptable alternative to "soon". Answers A, B, and D are all idiomatically correct (remember, idioms are difficult to

learn- you must rely on your sense of "does it sound right?"). The correct answer to the question is C because you'd say "as soon as I arrived", not "as soon after I arrived".

18.   This question tests punctuation. G is incorrect because a comma after "aunt" makes an inappropriate break in the flow of the sentence. H is wrong for a similar reason- a comma after "said" makes an inappropriate break in the sentence, too. Answer J is incorrect because semicolons should be used to separate two independent clauses and this sentence should be one continuous sentence. The way it says "My aunt said she had a gift for me" it would be very awkward to put a semi-colon after "said" because it would read like the end of one thought "my aunt said.", when "my aunt said" and "she had a gift for me" are one thought that needs to be connected. The correct answer is F because this area requires no punctuation- the sentence is one continuous thought and needn't be broken by punctuation.

19.   This question is yet another rhetorical skills question. A is incorrect because the statement "I was expecting my aunt to hand me a ring or a bracelet, or maybe an old book" gives no indication of what is going to happen next, just what the writer thought she might get from her aunt. Answer C is also wrong because this is just what she was expecting to get, not what she normally gets. D is incorrect because the statement doesn't at all indicate how close the narrator and her aunt are, it's just a list of gifts the narrator thought she might receive. The correct answer is B because the statement lists what the narrator thought she would get, and then there is a contrast when the sentence says "but instead she let me outside". If you were to delete the statement, you would lose the important information that establishes a contrast between conventional and unusual.

20.   This question tests idiom usage. G is incorrect because Rosie hasn't heard of them talking, she just heard them talk. H is incorrect because you shouldn't use the preposition "of" after must (idiom error), and Rosie hasn't heard about them talking, she heard them talking. J is incorrect because again, "of" should not be used after must. This is an idiom error. This is misleading because the commonly used conjunction "must've" is pronounced "must of" but is actually an abbreviation for "must have". While "must've" would be

correct, "most of" would not be. The correct answer is F, "must have", because is it is idiomatically correct.

21.   This question tests sentence structure, and asks you to pick the answer that makes the sentence grammatically incorrect. A is an incorrect answer choice. "After my aunt assured me that Rosie wouldn't snap or bite" can not stand alone- therefore, it is a dependent clause. "I reached down to stroke her neck, admiring her brown and tan carapace, or upper shell" is an independent clause because it can function on it's own as a sentence. Put together, you get a "dependent clause, independent clause" proper sentence structure. B is also not the correct answer for the same reason: "When my aunt assured me that Rosie wouldn't snap or bite" is a dependent clause, giving the entire sentence a proper sentence structure of "dependent clause, independent clause". D is incorrect for the same reason as A and B. "Once my aunt assured me that Rosie wouldn't snap or bite" is also a dependent clause, giving the sentence proper sentence structure. The only choice that disrupts the grammatically correct sentence structure is answer C because "my" creates an independent clause in the first half of a sentence: "My aunt assured me that Rosie wouldn't snap or bite". However, since the second part of the sentence is an independent clause as well, you would need something in between (see the English study guide for information on changing "independent clause, independent clause" to being grammatically correct) to make the sentence have proper sentence structure. Thus, answer C is the correct answer.

22.   Rhetorical skills are being tested in this question. It asks where you would most logically place the introduction of Rosie into the paragraph. To decide where to do this, you have to read the essay and see where the first mention of Rosie appears in the paragraph. G is incorrect because sentence 2 already mentions Rosie and it would be pointless to introduce her after she has already been mentioned. H, or after sentence 3, is also an inappropriate location because again, Rosie has been mentioned, and it's awkward since it's between two unrelated thoughts: "she was over a foot long and about seven inches high" and "as soon as my aunt...snap or bite". J is also incorrect because after sentence 4, the writer has already interacted with the tortoise and her aunt has talked about the tortoise. It wouldn't make sense logically to have an introduction of the tortoise after these events. The only location for the introduction that makes sense in the flow of the paragraph is after sentence 1 because sentence 1 says

"She pointed to a corner of the yard...a dandelion" makes a clear indication that the writer's aunt is drawing attention to the tortoise, and it would make sense to introduce Rosie immediately after this gesture. The two sentences would read "She pointed to a corner of the yard, where a tortoise was calmly munching a dandelion. 'This is Rosie,' she announced". The progression is logical, making choice F the correct answer.

23.   Punctuation is being tested in this question. A is incorrect because it improperly utilizes a colon. Recall from the study guide that colons are used to begin a list or a definition. You may think that you're defining what Rosie is, but for definition usage of the colon, you shouldn't have "is" in front of the colon in any case. Think of the colon as a synonym to "is". If you have a definition you would say "Rosie is blah blah blah", but you could also say "Rosie: blah blah blah". It is improper to have both, rendering A incorrect. Another reason A is incorrect is because it doesn't have a comma to set off the extra phrase "it turns out". Setting off additional phrases is covered in the study guide. Answer C is wrong because it too fails to set off the additional phrase "it turns out" because it doesn't place a coma after "out". Choice D is incorrect for the same reason, except in this case it has the comma after "out" but is lacking a comma before "it". B is the correct answer because it properly sets off the additional phrase "it turns out", and does not introduce any more grammatical errors.

24.   This question is testing a concept similar to misplaced modifiers, except later in the sentence. All the answer choices are technically grammatically correct. F, G, and J are all proper arrangements of words to fit the context of the sentence, and convey the idea that the writer's grandmother raised Rosie. However, H is incorrect. Put the phrase "started up raising" into the sentence. It reads, "Rosie, it turns out, is a desert tortoise that my grandmother had started up raising over twenty years ago". "Started up raising", in reference to Rosie, who is the subject of the sentence, makes it sound as if the writer's grandmother had started Rosie raising something of her own, as in the tortoise raising something herself. All the other arrangements (started raising, started to raise, and begun raising) are talking about the writer's grandmother, but the way H is arranged it's talking about Rosie raising something, which is clearly not the idea the writer wishes to convey. Also, do not confuse "started out" with "started up". If the option had been "started out", the sentence would

still be referencing the grandmother and would have made sense, but because it says "started up" it's talking about the subject, Rosie.

25.   For this question, time and tense are being tested, but not in a common way. Although they all make sense grammatically, three are incorrect because they create confusion in whether the writer's aunt has already asked about the writer caring for Rosie or not. A, or "would have checked" is implying that her aunt would have checked, but did not for some reason. However, since the latter part of the sentence talks about her parents agreeing, her aunt must have asked about the writer caring for the tortoise, making A wrong. C is also incorrect because "would check" implies that the writer's aunt has not yet checked with the parents, yet since the parents agreed she must have already checked. D is wrong for the same reason. "Must check" implies that the writer's aunt is planning on checking with the parents, but she has not yet, which again conflicts with the part of the sentence that says the parents are already okay with it. The only answer that supports the time frame of the author's parents' agreement is B ("had checked") because it implies that the writer's aunt has already checked with the parents, unlike all the other answer choices.

26.   Here's another rhetorical skills question. They ask you to pick the topic sentence that is most relevant to the content of the following paragraph. The first step is to read the paragraph, and then you can decide which of the options is most relevant. F is incorrect because no where in the paragraph is there any more information about the age relationship of the writer and Rosie. H is also incorrect because the paragraph doesn't talk about where tortoises are located in the world, it's talking about their shelter and food. J is wrong because the paragraph doesn't contain information about the tortoise's size. G is the correct answer because the paragraph talks about the tortoise's special housing and eating arrangements in respects to living in a human household, and that sort of information would follow if the author had asked her aunt about Rosie's needs.

27.   This question also tests rhetorical skills. Recall that often, though not always, the most concise answer is the correct one in the case of rhetorical skills question. A is long and contains superfluous information- "experience the satisfaction of contentment" is too wordy and irrelevant. Although B doesn't contain extra information, it is too long and there are easier, shorter ways to say the same thing, as

you'll see in choice D. C is insignificant information, since the author wants to write about the nutritional value, not the tortoise's level of contentment. D is the best answer because it's concise, and demonstrates nutritional value by saying "adequately nourished".

28.   This is a rhetorical skills question. The questions asks you to give the most specific example of other foods tortoises eat from the options given. G is certainly not the answer because when they're talking about what foods tortoises eat, obviously they are "things they could eat". H is also equally nebulous because of course, if the tortoise is eating it, it's edible. J is a little tricky, seeing as all the already listed foods fit into the category of fresh foods. However, F, or "vegetables and fruit", is more specific and all the listed items fit into that category too, so it is the correct answer.

29.   This question tests punctuation, specifically apostrophe usage. You have to remember what each location for an apostrophe means. The writer is trying to say each parent with their own backyard. B is incorrect because "parent's backyards" means one parent, multiple backyards. C is wrong because there is no apostrophe to even suggest possession- that is, that the parents own the backyards. D is incorrect for the same reason as C- it has no apostrophe. A is the correct answer because by putting the apostrophe after parents, you're saying multiple parents, each with their own backyard, which is what the author meant to say.

30.   This question tests idiom usage. F is incorrect because it uses the wrong preposition, "in". Is it really one of the most endangered families "in" reptiles? It's not really "in", like inside, reptiles. H is wrong because it uses "in" and because "family" should be plural. Though using family singularly can be grammatically correct, that is not what the author is trying to say. The author is trying to say that tortoises are a family of their own, not part of a bigger family, which is the only case in which you could use a singular "family" (it would read "I learned that tortoises are among the most endangered family in reptiles"). However, since this isn't the case, choice J also gets eliminated. The correct answer is G because it uses the correct preposition "of", as in part of the family, and also uses the plural "families", which indicates that tortoises make up a family of their own and that they are endangered. You might be wondering how you would know whether the author wanted the meaning derived from the singular "family" or

the meaning derived from the plural "families". Since the author hasn't mentioned any other animal or any bigger category for the tortoise to fit into, it is safe to assume that the author means to speak of tortoises themselves as one family.

31.   This question also tests punctuation. The author is trying to write of Benjamin Banneker's one family, that owns a farm. A is incorrect because putting the apostrophe after the "s" in"familys" would mean multiple families, which there aren't. In addition, "familys" isn't a word, since the plural of "family"is "families". C is also wrong for the first reason that A is wrong- putting the apostrophe after "families" would mean multiple families, when the author is talking about Benjamin Banneker's one family. D is incorrect because there is no apostrophe to indicate any possession at all, and you need an apostrophe somewhere to show that his family owns the farm. B is the correct answer because it places the apostrophe before the "s". In this manner, it shows possession of the farm and indicates one family.

32.   Misplaced modification is being tested in this question. Choices G, H, and J are all acceptable because they convey that Banneker had a difficult time getting a formal education. However, F does not. If you place F in the sentence, it reads "Though limiting his access to formal education, Banneker nevertheless demonstrated...acquiring knowledge." By using the word "limiting", it sounds as though Banneker was limiting his own opportunities in formal education. All the other choices avoid this modification error, making F incorrect.

33.   Who/whom rules are tested in this question. Remember that who goes with she, and whom goes with her. Who was the indentured servant? She (Banneker's grandmother) was. If you are confused as to how to differentiate who/whom, it is covered in more detail in the study guide. Since you can use "whom", A is wrong. C is also incorrect because "which" would refer to something other than a person. We use "who" and "whom" for people, while "which" is used for "it" rather than "he" or "she". D is wrong because in deleting the phrase you would lose the comma used to set off the phrase "after completing the term of her contract". See the study guide for information on setting off phrases. The correct answer is B because it uses who, which corresponds to she, and *she* was the indentured servant.

34.   Thirty-four is a rhetorical skills question. The question asks if you should add a sentence with an explanation of the "contract" that Banneker's grandmother had filled. This may be tempting, considering that it is on topic in comparison to the last sentence, which talks about Banneker's grandmother's contract. However, in order to properly answer this question you need to keep the information presented throughout the essay in mind. Knowing this, look at the choices available to you. F is incorrect because knowing "the extent of control that masters held over indentured servants" doesn't have much to do with any other information in the essay, which focuses on Banneker's accomplishments. G is incorrect because it isn't necessary to understanding the essay as a whole since indentured servants are not mentioned again, and are merely mentioned before just to give a brief background of Banneker's family. H is wrong because if you scan the essay, you'll see no such information mentioned anywhere else in the essay. J is the correct answer because this information does indeed distract the reader from the main topic of the essay , which is Banneker's accomplishments. The information is unrelated to the focus of the essay.

35.   This question tests punctuation. A is the wrong answer because a semi-colon effectively splits the two parts of the sentence (both of which are independent clauses) into the format "independent clause ; independent clause", which is grammatically correct. B is an incorrect because in between the independent clauses are a comma and a transition ("and"), which is another proper way to separate independent clauses. D is a wrong answer because it splits the two independent clauses into two sentences with the use of a period. The correct answer is C because by omitting punctuation in between "read" and "he", you create a run-on sentence.

36.   Rhetorical skills are being tested in this question. The question asks you to arrange the given facts in the most logical order. F is incorrect because Banneker displayed his mechanical skills and interest in learning by constructing the clock, and the way F is arranged, it seems as though all three are different events. G is incorrect because although it says "displayed his skills when he constructed...", after that it says "and displayed his interest in mechanical skills". This arrangement fails to make it apparent that Banneker displayed his interest in learning by making the clock, and the option makes it seem like "displaying his interest in mechanical skills" is a completely different event, unrelated to the construction of

the clock. J is also wrong- it has "his interest in learning" at the end. This arrangement doesn't imply that he displayed his interest in learning by making the clock, but as a different happening altogether. H is the correct answer because it places "displayed his interest in learning and his mechanical skills" before "constructed a clock...", and in doing so shows that he displayed his interest in learning and his mechanical skills when he built the clock.

37.   Punctuation is tested in this question. Here, you are trying to indicate possession- that is, the watch possessing components. A is incorrect because "it's" actually means it is, which isn't showing possession. Don't be fooled by the apostrophe in "it's"- it does NOT indicate possession in any circumstance. B is wrong because "its'" is not an existent word. D is wrong because, though it shows possession, "their" is plural and "pocket watch" is singular, so you can't use "their". C is the correct answer because "its" indicates possession in the singular form, which corresponds to "pocket watch" in number.

38.   This question tests tenses. F is incorrect because "keeps" is present tense, and the rest of the essay has been written in past tense, so you need a past tense verb. G is incorrect because it is in present perfect form, which doesn't specify that there is an endpoint. J is also a present tense verb so it is wrong for the same reason as F. H is the correct answer because it is in simple past tense form, which agrees with the tense of the rest of the essay.

39.   This is yet another rhetorical skills question. The question is testing how well you can maintain the tone of the essay. Looking through the essay, you'll see no mention of personal opinion, only facts. It maintains an impersonal perspective of Banneker's life, feeding only facts. Keeping this in mind, approach the answer choices. A, B, and C all uses phrases that indicate opinion ("can you believe it?", "amazing", "unbelievable"). D is the only choice that keeps the tone factual and non-opinionated.

40.   This question tests rhetorical skills. G, though grammatically correct, is the wrong answer because "therefore" would imply that it was because he took responsibility of the farm and family, he pursued scientific studies and taught himself to play instruments. This is not

the case, as he did the latter in addition to supporting his family. H is a comma splice error, making it an incorrect answer. J is also a comma splice, and it uses the wrong transition (therefore), so it is wrong. The correct answer is F, because it avoids the comma splice error and uses a logical transition (in addition), making it clear that Banneker pursued science and learned to play instruments, and he took care of his family, not that he took care of his family and as a result pursued science and learned to play instruments, which wouldn't make much sense.

41.   Rhetorical skills are tested in this question. B is incorrect because the previous passage makes no mention of musical interests, or any additional pursuits. C is the wrong answer because although it is a description of Banneker's interests, it is a relatively dry description. There are no words present in the phrase to imply humor. D is incorrect because the mention of playing the flute and violin isn't very extensive, as D doesn't go into more detail about Banneker's musical endeavors. The correct answer is A because the sentence talks about Banneker's other learning pursuits and teaching himself to play instruments is a fitting example of his will to learn.

42.   This is another rhetorical skills question, testing ambiguous pronoun reference. F, or "them", is incorrect because "them" could be the Sun, Moon, and other celestial bodies, or the paths. It is unclear what "them" is referring to. H is wrong for the same reason- "those" makes it unclear what exactly "those" are. J is incorrect because "these things" doesn't eliminate the uncertainty caused, just like in F and H. The correct answer is G because by saying "these calculations", there is a direct reference (the calculations) so we know what the sentence is talking about.

43.   Redundancy is tested in this question. Notice how the sentence says "annual tables", meaning yearly. A is incorrect because since you already have "annual", it is implied that they are "yearly". B is incorrect for the same reason- "annual" obviously covers a year's worth of data, so it's unnecessary to have both phrases. C is incorrect because "annual" is once every twelve months. A, B, and C are all redundant. D is the correct answer because it eliminates the redundancy by removing the phrase altogether.

44.   This is a rhetorical skills question. Consider which points have been stressed in the essay and the general information presented. The questions asks you to pick a statement that summarizes the essay well. F isn't a good choice because the essay barely mentioned that Banneker was the son of an indentured servant or that he liked to study music. G is also wrong because it is not a summary of all that Banneker did- it talks of specifically one thing that Banneker did with the pocket watch. This is not a good representation of the whole essay, as it was only mentioned once. H misses the whole point of the essay, not even listing one of Banneker's many accomplishments in the field of astronomy. J is the correct answer because it covers many of the things done by Banneker by saying "farmer, inventor, and self-taught mathematician and astronomer" and then put in the widely encompassing statement "took advantage of every opportunity to learn and contribute to the society of his time", which is applicable to each of the accomplishments mentioned in the essay.

45.   This is another rhetorical skills question. It asks where the most logical place to put paragraph five is. To do this, you must look at how the paragraph would transition with other paragraphs in context, and at the chronological order. B is incorrect because launching straight into his accomplishments after paragraph one and then going back to his roots is incongruous- all the background information should be together, and putting in paragraph five between paragraphs one and two would separate the background information. C is incorrect because if you look at the year in paragraph five, it says the year "1788" and because paragraph 3 says "1753", it wouldn't make sense to have paragraph five, which contains events that happen later, before paragraph three, which has events dating earlier. D is wrong because of the same reason- paragraph four contains events from 1759, and it wouldn't be chronologically proper to place that paragraph after a paragraph containing events from 1788. A is the correct answer because it chronologically maintains the order, and the flow of information is not choppy. By keeping the paragraph where it is, the essay assumes a structure in which background information about Banneker is given, followed by information about his accomplishments.

46.   Redundancy is being tested in this question. F is incorrect because wilderness areas are wild, hence them being called wilderness areas, so it is unnecessary to have both phrases there. G is incorrect because again, wilderness areas are of great remoteness,

and that is implied already. H is wrong because wilderness areas are called wilderness areas because they are uncivilized. Notice how all these unnecessary phrases in F, G, and H are subsets of the definition of wilderness itself, so you don't need to have them in the sentence as wilderness already implies them. The correct answer is J because of this; the phrases are not needed.

47.   This question tests agreement. A is incorrect because "it" is singular and "kayaks" is plural. B is incorrect because "one" would be referring to one kayak, and you're talking about multiple kayaks. D is incorrect because "which are" would make the sentence a dependent clause, and dependent clauses cannot stand alone. The correct answer is C because "they" is plural like "kayaks" is, so it agrees.

48.   This is a rhetorical skills question. F is incorrect because that sentence doesn't distinguish types of kayaks, it just gives you a little information about the structure. H is incorrect because the sentence is pertinent to the preceding sentence about materials- the first sentence of the paragraph talks about materials, and the second says that those materials cover everything but the opening for seating. J is incorrect because the sentence doesn't seem awkwardly wordy, it's a normal sentence that is easy to read. G is the correct answer because the sentence helps the reader envision what a kayak loos like.

49.   Punctuation is tested in this question. A is incorrect because to use a semi-colon, you need two independent clauses, and "the easily maneuverable...sea kayak" is a dependent clause. B is wrong because there shouldn't be a comma between "kayaks" and "are" since no break is necessary there. D is wrong because a dash is unnecessary here since again, no break is needed. The correct answer is C because there is no punctuation necessary.

50.   This question tests agreement in a little bit of a different way. F is incorrect because since you're talking about types of kayak, saying "largest" could possibly imply a singular "biggest" boat, and since you're just trying to say it's larger in comparison to the white-water kayak, you cannot use a superlative. G is wrong for exactly the same reason as F. H and J are more difficult. For one syllable adjectives/adverbs (in this case, large), you would use an -er ending. For adjectives/adverbs of two syllables or more, you would use "more"

followed by that word. This applies to comparatives with adverbs/adjectives which do not end in -y. Since large has one syllable, you would say "larger" rather than "more large". Therefore, H is incorrect and J is correct. This seems like a very specific rule, and it should be noted that in all the ACT examinations I have analyzed, I haven't come across any such question testing this concept. In the context of the sentence, given the options "larger" and "more large", for most people "larger" just seems to sound better, and it is not worth memorizing such a specific rule- if you have a strong feeling that one flows better than the other, you can go with it. However, for those of you who have trouble distinguishing what is correct by the sound of it in this context, it is worth making a note of this rule so that you do not have this problem in the future.

51.   Punctuation is tested in this question. A is incorrect because it has no punctuation, making it a run-on sentence. B is incorrect because it uses a semi-colon incorrectly- the first half of the sentence should be an independent clause, and "Kayaking in white water" is a dependent clause. D is incorrect because a comma is needed between "water" and "the". C is the correct answer because the comma after "water"sets off the phrase "the tumultuous rapids of swift-moving rivers", which is a description of "white water".

52.   Rhetorical skills are tested in question fifty-two. F is incorrect because "at last" would mean the final step in something, and the preceding sentences don't mention any process or steps. G is incorrect because "for example" would be giving support to something in the preceding sentences, but the fact that kayakers are advised to wear safety equipment doesn't support the preceding point that kayaks are stable and unlikely to capsize. H is incorrect for the same reason. Using "therefore" would imply that because kayaks are stable, kayakers must wear safety equipments, and those statements contradict each other so it doesn't make sense to use "therefore". J is the correct answer because since the statements are contradictory, you have to use a transition that shows contradiction, and "nevertheless" does that.

53.   This is also a rhetorical skills question. A is an incorrect answer because "thus" implies that the latter part of the sentence happens because of the preceding part of the sentence, which is what using "so" does, and since you're looking for an alternative, to "so"

"thus" is fine. B is also a wrong answer because "consequently" makes a good replacement for "so" for the same reason as "thus". C is incorrect for the same reasons as A and B. D is the correct answer because "yet" implies contrast, and you want a cause-effect transition like "so", not one that shows contrast.

54.   This is a rhetorical skills question. The question specifically asks which choice is most relevant to the material at the end of the sentence. G is incorrect because person is unspecific, as person can be used in any situation. There are more specific choices. H is incorrect because although the person is paddling in the boat, there is a choice that is more specific to the end of the sentence, which talks about wildlife and shorebirds. J is also pretty non-specific and can be used in a variety of situations, so it is incorrect. The best answer is F because "nature watcher" directly correlates to the latter part of the sentence. It is important to note that although all the wrong choices are acceptable alternatives, you have to chose the most pertinent answer from your options.

55.   This is another rhetorical skills question. To answer this, you have to find a sentence that is specific to one type of kayak. A is incorrect because it talks about kayaks in general, not specifically about one type of kayak. B is incorrect because it isn't specific to one type of kayak. In fact, it is talking about the kayakers, not even the kayaks. D is incorrect because again, it doesn't talk specifically about one of the types of kayaks: white water and sea. C is the correct answer because it is the only choice that is specific to one type of kayak, the sea kayak, making it a good candidate for starting a discussion about sea kayaks.

56.   This questions tests parallelism. F is incorrect because "are" is plural, and "equipment" is singular. Keep in mind "equipment" is the noun you want to match, not "kayaks". H is incorrect because "were" is past tense, and you are talking in the present, and it's plural and "equipment" is singular. J is incorrect because though "was" is singular, it is past tense and you want to stay in present tense. The correct answer is G because "is" is present tense and singular, just like "equipment".

57.   This question tests sentence structure and transitions. A is incorrect because if you just left it as "paddle,", the sentence would have a comma splice. C is wrong because the transition "so" is not used properly. "So" is used for cause and effect scenarios, and since the two parts of the sentence ("Kayakers use a short, double-bladed paddle" and "an elasticized sprayskirt...") don't have a cause-effect relationship, you can't use "so". D is incorrect because using "paddle" without any punctuation and transition would give you a run-on sentence. The correct answer is B because it uses a comma followed by a transition ("and", meaning something else in addition) to employ proper sentence structure.

58.   Fifty-eight is a rhetorical skills question. F is incorrect because the way it is placed, it sounds as if you're pulling one end through the water of the paddle, as if it's the paddle's own water. G is incorrect because putting the phrase after "paddler" makes it seem as if the paddler is through the water, and not the end of the paddle. H is incorrect because "The paddler pulls through the water" almost sounds like the paddler pulls himself/herself through the water. It's similar to the phrase "you can pull through this", yet that's not what you want to get across. J is the correct answer because by placing the phrase after "paddle", you make the phrase "one end of the paddle"instead of separating it, and it is made clear the the end of the paddle is being pulled through the water.

59.   This questions test punctuation. A is incorrect because no comma is needed after "simple". "Simple but versatile" is one phrase. C is incorrect because of the same reason- "simple but versatile" shouldn't be broken by a dash. D is also wrong for the same reasons as A and C. The semicolon is used incorrectly in D. If you are confused about the uses of these punctuations, review their uses in the study guide. B is the correct answer because it has no punctuation, and punctuation is not necessary in this phrase.

60.   This is another rhetorical skills question. F is incorrect because the paragraph says "upper-body muscles" and that's as much detail as it goes into about which muscles are used to propel a kayak. H is incorrect because the paragraph doesn't go into the science of how water moves around a kayak, only that there are "nuances of the water", and that isn't scientific. J is wrong because no where in the paragraph do they ask the kayakers to be careful about the

environment. The paragraph does mention, however, the efforts of the kayakers and their relationship with the water and what they do in the kayak. The paragraph intertwines the kayakers, kayak, and water, so G is correct.

61.   Punctuation is tested in this question. A is incorrect because there shouldn't be a semicolon between "rock" and "miles", as that is not the proper use of a semicolon. B is incorrect because a comma between "seams" and "of" is unnecessary. D is wrong because of the same reason as B- there is no need for a comma between "seams" and "of". Furthermore, D is incorrect because of the comma after "rock", which isn't needed. C is the correct answer because no punctuation is needed in this sentence.

62.   This question tests sentence structure. F is incorrect because putting a period after the independent clause "Others, salt-encrusted, 'sleep; in ancient caverns" makes it a sentence. If you add "then they wake" to "after centuries to feed and to be bred", it makes another whole sentence, so F is an acceptable alternative. G is wrong because adding a transition (and then) makes proper sentence structure. H is wrong for the same reason as G, because of the transition (only to). The correct answer is J because "waking after centuries to feed and to be bred" is a dependent clause and cannot stand alone as its own sentence.

63.   Parallel structure (in this case, tense) is tested in this question. A is incorrect because the underlined phrase should resemble the structure of "to feed" (the infinitive), so it should read "to breed". B is incorrect because it too is in the wrong tense- the phrase should have the infinitive structure (to feed) to maintain parallelism. D is incorrect because of the same reason: it is in the wrong tense. The correct answer is C because it is in infinitive form, just like "to feed".

64.   This is a rhetorical skills question. You want to pick the least wordy option and best flowing option, since all of them are actually grammatically correct, and it has to suit the tone of the passage. F and G are wordy and sound too basic for the tone of the passage. J doesn't suit the tone of the paragraph at all. The correct answer is H because it fits the tone of the passage and keeps the same slightly more professional sound that the other options fail to hold. Plus, the

usage of "still" is a good way to say "even more", which is what the author wants to get across.

65.   Punctuation is tested in this question, as well as correct usage of "to". A is incorrect because it uses the wrong "to"- it should use "too" to indicate too much. C is incorrect because there is no need for a comma after "poisonous", since you don't want to set off the phrase "to sustain life". D is incorrect because it uses "to", instead of "too", which you need to indicate "too much". The correct answer is B because it uses the correct "too" and doesn't put a comma after "poisonous".

66.   This is another question that tests punctuation. In this sentence you want to set off the parenthetical expression "called extremophiles", because otherwise you would have a run-on. F is incorrect because to set off the expression "called extremophiles", you would need a comma after survivors. H is incorrect because by not putting a comma after "extremophiles", it fails to set off the phrase "called extremophiles". J is wrong because the semicolon at the end of "extremophiles" is used improperly- there shouldn't be a semicolon there. The correct answer is G because it sets off the parenthetical expression "called extremophiles" by placing commas before and after.

67.   This question also tests punctuation. A is incorrect because it employs the proper usage of the semicolon by putting it between two independent clauses. B is incorrect because it uses the dash properly, also by putting it between two independent clauses. C is also the wrong answer because it separates the two independent clauses by putting a period in between. D is the correct answer because by not putting any punctuation between "forms" and "they", it creates a run-on sentence.

68.   This question tests tense. The tense of this essay is present, so you'll want to maintain that throughout. F is incorrect because it is in past tense. G is incorrect because the tense is past progressive. H is incorrect because the tense is past perfect. The correct answer is J because the tense is present, which matches the tense of the rest of the essay.

69.   This is a rhetorical skills question. Pick the option that is concise and best gets the point across without digression. A is incorrect because it is not necessary to go into detail about what geysers are in Yellowstone since you're just talking about the thermal pools as a whole. B is incorrect because you don't need to introduce a contrast at all, especially if the thing being contrasted hasn't been mentioned previously. Since the "cool depths of Scandinavian fjords" are a completely new topic in this paragraph, there's no need for a contrast, and in this case it is an unnecessary digression that lead's the readers attention away from the thermal pools of Yellowstone. C is incorrect because the tone of the phrase is not suiting to the essay; in particular, the term "geologic magic" is far too unprofessional sounding for the rest of the essay. D is the correct answer because it shortens the phrase to just "pools", eliminating digressions and keeping the focus strictly on the thermal pools in which extremophiles live.

70.   Seventy is a rhetorical skills question. F is incorrect because it's not saying that extremophiles live in two different places, the Pacific Ocean and the Juan de Fuca Ridge, it's saying that there is a specific location within the Pacific Ocean called Juan de Fuca Ridge. H is incorrect because the preceding paragraph doesn't say anything about how thermophiles only live in water. Plus, paragraph three doesn't contradict that statement anyway, seeing as the thermophiles described live in water. J is incorrect because if you look at the rest of the passage, you'll see this information isn't present later in the text. The correct answer is G because in the next sentence there is a "here" that will need a location to refer to, and by cutting out the information about where these thermophiles are, the "here" won't have a location to describe.

71.   This is another rhetorical skills question. B is incorrect because although it says "there are signs of both seismic and volcanic activity", it does not expand on what these "signs" are. C is incorrect because like in B, it says "the results of earthquakes and volcanic eruptions are evident", but doesn't say more about such "results", which would give us more information about what exactly the ocean floor looks like. D is incorrect for the same reason as B and C- "the effect" mentioned is not explained in more depth. The correct answer is A because it gives an actual description of the ocean floor's coverings- "scarred by earthquakes and underwater volcanoes" is a specific description, which other options lack.

72.   Seventy-two is also a rhetorical skills question. F is incorrect because after "waters", it seems like the "cracks" temperatures are up to 360 degrees Celsius, and not the water. G is incorrect because the temperatures do not come from the cracks, as this placement implies. H is incorrect because all though the water does come from the cracks, it would be better to have a verb that describes how the water is moving from the cracks. Thus, J is the best answer because it uses the verb "gush" before "from cracks", making it clearer how the water moved.

73.   Here's a rhetorical skills question. B is incorrect because it does transition from the last paragraph about thermophiles by mentioning them. C is incorrect for the same reason- it says "rather than hot ones", introducing a contrast that blends the preceding paragraph into this one. D is also wrong because it says "other types", demonstrating a contrast from the thermophiles, and works as a transition. The least transitioning option is A, because it mentions nothing about thermophiles, nor does it mention any contrast, so there is no transition period.

74.   This is a rhetorical skills question. F is incorrect because the part of the sentence right after "if life can persist in extreme environments on Earth" talks about how there could be life elsewhere. H is incorrect because that statement makes no contradictions that life exists in extreme environments; it is saying itself that "life can persist in extreme environments", so it is clearly not implying that life can't exist in harsh environments. J is wrong because rather than digressing into a different topic (namely, life on Earth), the clause acts as a transition into a speculation about extraterrestrial life. A clue is the "if" in "if life can persist" because you know of the "if-then" relationship and you know a "then" statement is coming, which in this case is "life may endure...elsewhere". The correct answer is G because of the "if-then" relationship in the phrase, explained above.

75.   This question tests transitions. A, B, and C are all incorrect because those are transitions that imply contrast. Since the last paragraph talks about life elsewhere, and so does this paragraph, there shouldn't be a contrast transition because both paragraphs are supporting the same opinion. D is the correct answer because it is a transition that reinforces the given topic, rather than implying contrast.

ACT MATH CONCEPTS
By **Rajiv Raju**

Key Math Strategies:

*-**Get it right the first time**. Going back to check your work usually does not help on the ACT since you will probably make the same errors the second time. You will score higher by spending more time on one pass as opposed to rushing though the problem twice.*

*-**Write a lot on the test booklet.** The more you write, draw, and label the more likely you are to get the correct answer. On geometric problems, label every angle and side you can deduce from the information given. If there is formula involved, write the formula or equation down. **Do not try to solve problems in your head**. This will slow you down and increase the chance of error. Draw tables, charts, or sketches to help you organize your thinking about long word problems. See Question 56.*

*-**Never struggle with a problem.** If you are having any trouble with a problem, just guess and go on to the next problem. Most people will be better off by being careful on the problems they can solve rather than struggling with difficult problems that they will probably get wrong anyway. If you happen to have time to go back, spend time on the problems that you have the best chance of answering correctly.*

*-**On difficult geometry questions, guess based on your intuition and visual estimation from the diagram.** Unlike the SAT, all figures on the ACT are to scale. You may not always be able to guess the right answer, but you may be able to eliminate some wrong choices. See Question 43.*

*-**Do not overuse the calculator.** Unlike the SAT, the ACT often will have answers listed as fractions and radicals. Some answers will have π in them. In these cases, if you do everything on the calculator you will not find the answer on your calculator. See questions 31, 38, 41 and 44.*

*-Reading mistakes are the most common type of mistake on the math test. Every word in the question matters. You should have a clear understanding of the math vocabulary used in the problem. Make sure you actually answer the question that is asked. **<u>Try to underline the key phrase that indicates what the test makers want. Make it a habit to reconfirm that you answered what was asked before you fill in the answer.</u>** This only takes a second, but will decrease your errors significantly. See Questions 29 and 33.*

-Do not look for tricks on the ACT, but think carefully. The standard classroom approach of solving the problems will usually work on the ACT. The very evil and tricky questions sometimes seen on the SAT are absent from the ACT, although the wrong answer choices on the ACT will often be the most common mistakes that students tend to make.

*-In some problems it may be faster and easier to work backwards from the answer choices and plug the answers in to the problem. If you try this, **try the middle answer choice first** and try to eliminate as many wrong answers as possible with each try. Do not get carried away with this technique, since most questions can be answered faster with the standard classroom approach. See Questions 18 and 44.*

-Sometimes it is possible to answer the question after only performing part of the calculation. This can save you time. See Question 9.

-You need to memorize a few important formulas. Unlike the SAT there is no formula list on the test. All the formulas that you need to memorize are in this chapter. Less important formulas (commonly, the law of sines and cosines) are usually given as part of the question. See Questions 31 and 41.

*-You may never need to use the graphing capabilities of your calculator since no problem absolutely requires this capability, but a graphing calculator can sometimes be **used for an alternative approach.** See Question 21.*

A comprehensive review of the mathematical concepts needed for the ACT is beyond the scope of this book. The vast majority of the questions only require middle school math, Algebra I and Geometry. There are some questions that deal with more advanced Algebra II concepts. Trigonometry is tested but there are no more than 4 questions on a typical test. At least two of these questions only deal with simple right triangle ratios and can be answered if you know the definitions of the trigonometric ratios. Advanced knowledge of trigonometry is not necessary to get a good math score.

In general, on the ACT Math section, when advanced concepts are tested they are often tested in simple straight-forward questions. Do not underestimate the importance of basic concepts and skills, which are often tested in more unusual ways.

The brief listing below is intended to emphasize the most important topics that are tested and to direct the reader to real ACT questions that test the concept. The list also includes formulas that you should know. It is very important to see how the concepts are tested on real test questions because the ACT places great emphasis on the application of concepts rather than rote memorization. **The most effective way to prepare for the ACT math is to practice and analyze as many _real_ test questions as possible.**

The practice test in the booklet is only a start. You should also analyze the two additional real practice tests that are available free. For detailed instructions about how to get these free tests, see the second chapter in this book. Although the ACT test will have different questions each time, the same concepts and thinking skills tend to be tested repeatedly. By studying the three tests, you will learn the most important skills and concepts need to do well on the test. As you practice, try to come up with your own strategies to improve speed and accuracy.

Even when students understand the concepts, they often get the wrong answer because of carelessness. Common sources of error on the ACT math include not reading the question carefully and trying to solve the problem mentally instead of writing out the calculation or drawing a diagram. The more information you put down on paper, the more likely you are not to make an error.

Comparison with the SAT Math

The knowledge and skills tested on the SAT and ACT are similar, but there are also substantial differences. All of the math knowledge tested on the SAT is also tested on the ACT, but the ACT also tests additional topics not tested on the SAT. These additional topics include Trigonometry, Logarithms and Conic Sections. A typical test will have 4 trigonometry questions, one or no logarithm questions, and one or no conic section questions. If Logarithm and Conics questions are on the test, they will usually be quite basic. The questions on the ACT also tend to be more straightforward then the SAT, but the ACT gives you less time to do the questions.

Unlike the SAT math test, ACT math test often lists answer choices only in radical and fractional form. In these cases you should not do the whole problem on the calculator, since your calculator will give a decimal answer which will not match up with the answer choices.

Also unlike the SAT, there is no list of formulas at the beginning of the test. The ACT expects you to know the most important formulas such as, area formulas for circles, triangles and quadrilaterals. The listing below includes the formulas that you are expected to memorize. Less important formulas (like volume of a cylinder) are usually provided

with the question. On the SAT math the easy questions come first and the hard questions come last. This is not the case on the ACT math where there is no order of difficulty. You should never waste time on an ACT question that you are having trouble with. Just guess and go to the next question. Otherwise you may not have the opportunity to answer easy questions that may come later in the test. The ACT math test also gives you less time per question than the SAT. The ACT gives 60 seconds per math question, while the SAT gives you 75 seconds per math question. You should also be aware that the **TI-89 calculator**, which is permitted on the SAT, is **not permitted on the ACT**.

Pre-Algebra/Basic Math

Basic arithmetic is usually not directly tested. But many word problems only require translation of the problem to a basic arithmetic calculation. Almost a quarter of the test is devoted to pre algebra and basic math. Do not take these questions lightly, since it is possible to make difficult questions from simple concepts.

Some questions will test your understanding of basic math vocabulary. You should have a clear understanding of words like **factor, multiple, integer, real number,** etc.

Be careful to note subtle differences between words like positive (does not include 0) and non negative (includes 0).

Tables or graphs of information and numbers will be provided and you will be expected to answer questions based on the information in the table or graph. These questions usually do not require advanced mathematical concepts, but only require careful interpretation of tables or graphs and performing basic arithmetic calculations.

See: Questions 13, 14, 15, 19, 42 and 45

Order of Operations

You should be familiar with how to enter expressions into your calculator so that the operations are performed in the correct order.

See: Question 1

It helps to memorize the squares and cubes of the first few numbers. This will make answering some questions much faster and easier. For example, if you see $x^3=64$ on the test you should know x=4 without having to reach for the calculator. *Question 45.*

Squares: $2^2=4$, $3^2=9$, $4^2=16$, $5^2=25$, $6^2=36$, $7^2=49$, $8^2=64$, $9^2=81$, $10^2=100$, $11^2=124$, $12^2=144$

Cubes: $2^3=8$, $3^3=27$, $4^3=64$, $5^3=125$, $6^3=216$

Fraction, Decimal, Percent and Ratio Arithmetic

You should be able to add, subtract, multiply, divide and convert fraction and decimal percent quantities as well as deal with ratios. Questions containing these concepts are usually word problems.

Average Problems

The average of n numbers is the sum of all of these numbers dived by n. If you know the average of a set of n numbers, you usually do not know what the individual numbers are, but you can determine what the sum of all the numbers in the set is. Sum of all n numbers in the set = n x average. Calculating the sum of all the numbers is often a good way to attack ACT average problems.

Do not fall for the weighted average trap. If there are 10 girls and 15 boys in a class, and the average for the girls on a test is 90 and the average for the boys is 80, what is the average score for the whole class? If you said 85 you fell for the trap! If you used the method suggested in the previous paragraph you would get the correct answer of 84. Total of scores for girls is 10x90=900. The total of scores for boys is15x 80=1200. Total of scores for class = 900+1200=2100. Average for whole class of 25 students is 2100/25=84.

See: Question 47

Simple Descriptive Statistics

You should understand the concepts of **mean** (average), **mode** (most common) and **median** (middle value).

Distance and Time Problems

You should know how to use the formula that relates time, distance and speed. On the ACT these are usually word problems.

Distance =Speed x Time

Simple Probability

These will often be word problems.

Probability=(number of favorable outcomes)/(total number of outcomes).

See: Questions 51

Counting

To calculate the total number of ways things can be combined you simply multiply the number of possible choices for each category.

Example: If you have 3 types of shoes, 5 types of shirts, and 7 types of pants. The total number of ways that you

can combine these is 3x5x7=105

See: Questions 28

Elementary Algebra

Distributive property: a (b+c-d) =ab+ac-ad

Combining like terms.

See: Question 4

FOIL :(4z+3)(z-2) = 4z²-5z-6

See: Questions 6

Solving for one Variable in one Equation

You may be given one equation with two variables and asked to solve for one of the variables in terms of the other.

You may be given an equation with two variables and asked to determine the value of an expression with those two variables. In these questions you should not try to solve for one variable. You should manipulate the equation so one side of the equation looks like the expression that they ask you to evaluate. Example: a=b+10 what does 2(a-b) equal? a-b=10 so 2(a-b)=20. Though manipulations such as these may require some algebraic insight, practicing the manipulation method on several *real* ACT problems of this nature will make them a piece of cake.

Using a Given Formula

Some questions will give you a formula and ask you to answer a question that uses the formula. Make sure you perform the calculations using the correct order of operations and make sure you use the correct units.

See: Question 30

Some questions may require you to perform simple algebraic manipulations on a given a formula.

You will be expected to translate a verbal description to an algebraic expression.

Translating word problems to simple Algebra

This is one of the most common types of question on the ACT math.

See: Questions 2, 3 , 7, 8, 18, 20 ,24, and 27

Rationalizing the denominator

ACT often lists the answers in radical form with a rationalized denominator. You should know that:

$$\frac{1}{\sqrt{x}} = \frac{\sqrt{x}}{x}$$

(For those of you who didn't know, you get the expression on the right by multiplying the numerator and denominator by √X to get rid of the square root in the denominator)

See: Question 26

Intermediate Algebra

You should memorize the equations for difference of squares and perfect square binomial

$$A^2-B^2 = (A-B)(A+B)$$
$$(A + B)^2 = A^2 + 2AB+B^2$$
$$(A- B)^2 = A^2 -2AB+B^2$$

Factoring quadratic equations may be needed to simplify expressions by canceling the common factors. Usually the factoring will not be very difficult.

Solving quadratic equations by factoring. Usually the factoring will not be difficult. Set each factor equal to zero and solve.

See: Questions 21

You should be familiar with **function notation** and be able to evaluate functions. If $f(x) =x^2$ then $f(-3)=9$.

See: Questions 53 and 59

You should be able make **composite functions**. If $f(x)=x^2$ and $g(x)=3x+2$ what is $f(g(x))$?

$f(g(x))=f(3x+2)= (3x+2)^2$

See: Questions 32

Absolute Value

The concept of absolute value often tested. In these cases always test your answer in the question to make sure that you did not make an error.

| -5 | = 5 and | 5 | = 5

See: Questions 1 and 46

Inequalities

You will be expected to perform basic algebraic manipulations on inequalities.

See: Question 36

You should also be able to graph inequalities.

See: Question 57

Properties of exponents

Remember that these rules only work for the terms of the same base.

$$(x^n)(x^m)=x^{(n+m)}$$
$$(x^n)/(x^m)=x^{(n-m)}$$
$$(x^n)^m=x^{nm}$$

See: Questions 22, 35 and 49

Matrices

Sometimes the ACT may have one matrix question. They usually involve very simple matrix operations. Adding and subtracting matrices involves just adding or subtracting the corresponding elements in the matrix. Multiplication of very simple matrices may occasionally show up on the ACT.

See: Question 11

Logarithms

ACT occasionally tests this concept. Logarithmic notation is just a different way to express exponents. If you are more familiar with exponents then you may want to convert the problem to exponent notation.

$$\log_b A = E \text{ is the same thing as } b^E = A$$

Coordinate Geometry

Quadrant 1: value of x and y coordinates is positive

Quadrant 2: value of x is negative and values of y is positive

Quadrant 3: value of x and y coordinates is negative

Quadrant 4: value of x coordinates is positive and value of y coordinate is negative.

See: Question 23

Given two points (x_1,y_1) and (x_2,y_2) you should be able to calculate the slope of the line.

$$slope = \frac{y_2 - y_1}{x_2 - x_1}$$

All lines that have the same slope are parallel. If a line has slope m, then a line perpendicular to this line has slope -1/m.

You should be able to use the **slope intercept form** of an equation in two variables.

Y=mX + b   m=slope, b= Y intercept

See: Questions 17 and 52

You may be given equations for two lines and asked the coordinates of where they intersect. It may be faster to plug in the answers into both of the equations to see which answer works.

You are expected to know and use the **mid point formula**. An easy way to remember the formula is to see that coordinates of the midpoint are the average of coordinates of two points.

Given two points (x_1,y_1) and (x_2,y_2) the midpoint (x_m,y_m) is:

$$x_m = \frac{x_1 + x_2}{2}$$

$$y_m = \frac{y_1 + y_2}{2}$$

See: Question 9

You should know the **distance formula**. The distance between two points (x_1, y_1) and (x_2, y_2) is:

$$D = \sqrt{(x_2 - x_1)^2 + (y_2 - y_1)^2}$$

The ACT has an occasional question about parabolas, circles and ellipses. These only require a very basic understanding of the equations for these relations.

A **parabola** opening upward with vertex at origin:

$$y = x^2$$

The circle is the most commonly tested conic section on the ACT.

A **circle** with radius **r** and center **(h,k)** :

$$(x-h)^2 + (y-k)^2 = r^2$$

See: Questions 37 and 55

An **ellipse** with center (h,k) , horizontal axis 2a and vertical axis 2b

$$\frac{(x-h)^2}{a^2} + \frac{(y-k)^2}{b^2} = 1$$

Sequences

Arithmetic Sequences- each pair of successive terms differs by the same amount.

Example: 0, 5, 10,15, 20, 25, 30…. a difference between successive terms of 5

Most sequence questions can be answered by writing out about 5 terms and looking for a pattern. The question may be in to form of a word problem.   Usually, if there are a manageable number of terms, it is to your advantage to write out the sequence. **Don't trust just your brain's ability to visualize patterns, trust your brain and your eyes!** As Albert Einstein so eloquently stated: "The pencil adds 30 points to your IQ…" Use your pencil, especially for these types of problems!

See: Question 60

Plane Geometry

Distance between points on a line. You may be given multiple points on a line segment along with the distance between some of these points. You may be asked to figure out the distance between a set of points.
Example:

A   B C   D

AD=30 and AC=16 what is BC?

In problems like this, it is very useful to label the given distances on the picture.

Angles

You should be able to find angles based on given information. Listed below are come common geometric properties that are useful for finding angles on the ACT.

-Angles of a triangle add up to 180^C

-Corresponding angles of similar and congruent triangles are congruent. Triangles are similar if they have two angles that are congruent to each other.

See: Question 12

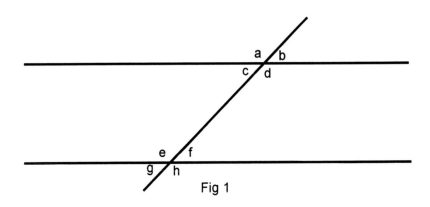

Fig 1

-Adjacent angles that form straight line will add up to 180^0.
*In Fig 1 **a+b=180⁰, b+d=180⁰, c+d=180⁰**, ect.*

-Vertical angles are congruent.
*In Fig 1 **a=d, c=b, f=g and e=h**.*

-Corresponding angels and alternate interior angles formed by transversals and parallel lines are congruent.

When a transversal crosses two parallel lines eight angles are formed. All of the acute angles are equal to each other and all of the obtuse angles are equal to each other. In Fig1 a=e=h=d and b=c=f=g

See: Questions 3 and 39

Triangles

Triangles Properties are tested quite often. If you have had geometry they should not be difficult. The special properties of **similar, isosceles, equilateral and right triangles** are especially popular on the test.

See: Questions 5, 12, 16 and 25

You should know the formula **for area of triangle:**

A= (1/2)bh where b=base and h=height

See: Question 59

Triangle Congruence

If two triangles are congruent, then corresponding angles and sides of the two triangles are equal to each other. Congruence can be shown by establishing congruence of these elements of the triangles:

SSS (side,side,side)

SAS (side,angle,side)

AAS(angle,angle, side)=**SAA** (side, angle, angle)

ASA (angle,side,angle)

AAA Does not establish congruence, but establishes similarity

ASS=SAA Does not establish congruence.

Pythagorean Theorem

$Leg1^2 + Leg2^2 = Hypotenuse^2$

Questions that use the Pythagorean Theorem are on every ACT. To decrease the chance of error and increase speed, it may be a good idea "pre solve" this equation for the hypotenuse and each of the legs. This way you will not make common mistakes like forgetting to take the square root to find the length of a side. When asked to calculate the leg or hypotenuse you can use these two forms of this equation.

$$leg_1 = \sqrt{hyp^2 - leg_2^2}$$
$$hyp = \sqrt{leg_1^2 + leg_2^2}$$

It is worth memorizing these two Pythagorean triples because they save you time and decrease chance of error.

3 : 4 : 5

5 : 12 : 13

You should also know the ratios for sides of the 45-90-45 and 30-60-90 right triangles.

45-90-45 : $1 : \sqrt{2} : 1$

30-60-90 : $1 : \sqrt{3} : 2$

Some word problems require the use of the Pythagorean Theorem.

See: Question 38

You should be able to calculate **perimeter and area** of common objects. Some questions require you to translate words to a figure and then calculate.

See: Question 5

Perimeter of rectangle= 2 (length + width)

Parallelograms

You will be expected to know the formula for the **area of a parallelogram**.

A=bh; where b=base and h=height

You will be expected to know the special properties of **isosceles trapezoid.**

See: Question 43

Areas of other polygons

On the ACT you can usually find areas of other polygons like trapezoids by adding area of rectangles and triangles.

It is worth memorizing the formula for the sum of the interior angles of a convex polygon.

Sum of interior angles of polygon of n sides = (n-2)x180

Circle Properties

You are expected to know formulas for **area and circumference.**

$$A = \pi r^{2}$$

$$C = 2\pi r$$

You will need to determine measurements for parts of circle. For example if the circumference of an entire circle is 100 then the length of a 60 degree sector is (60/360)x100=16.667.

A radius drawn to the point of tangency is perpendicular to the tangent.

A radius drawn perpendicular to a chord always bisects the chord.

Solid Geometry

Some questions dealing with solid objects will give you the needed formula, but you will be expected to know simple formulas such as the **volume a box= length x width x height.**

You should also be able to calculate areas of boxes. Formulas for things like volumes of cylinders are usually given in the problem. It is not necessary to memorize obscure solid geometry formulas, but if you are given a formula you should be able to use it to answer the question.

See: Questions 29 and 31

Trigonometry

There are no more that 4 trigonometry questions on a typical ACT test. Most of these do not need advanced knowledge. If you learn the definitions given below and learn how to use them, you have good chance of correctly answering two or three of these questions.

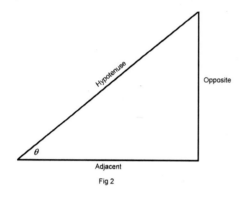

Fig 2

$$\sin \theta = \frac{opposite\_side}{hypotenuse}$$

$$\cos \theta = \frac{adjacent\_side}{hypotenuse}$$

$$\tan \theta = \frac{opposite\_side}{adjacent\_side}$$

$$\csc \theta = \frac{hypotenuse}{opposite} = \frac{1}{\sin \theta}$$

$$\sec \theta = \frac{hypotenuse}{adjacent} = \frac{1}{\cos \theta}$$

See: Questions 38 and 53

Also worth memorizing is:

$$\tan\theta = \frac{\sin\theta}{\cos\theta}$$

Notice that **if you know any two of these ratios, you can figure out all five of the ratios**.

The **Pythagorean identity** is worth memorizing for the ACT.

$$(\sin x)^2 + (\cos x)^2 = 1$$

Solve this for sin x and cos x to get:

$$\sin x = \sqrt{1-(\cos x)^2}$$
$$\cos x = \sqrt{1-(\sin x)^2}$$

When ever you see $\text{Sin}(x)^2 + \text{Cos}(x)^2$ you can replace it by 1 to simplify the expression.

Also if you see $\sqrt{1-(\cos x)^2}$ you can replace it by Sin(x).

Similarly $\sqrt{1-(\sin x)^2}$ can be replaced by Cos(x).

You are not expected to memorize a large number of obscure trigonometric identities, but you may be given an identity and asked to use it to answer the question. These questions can be answered by applying the rules of algebra to the given identity.

See: Question 41

Graphs of trigonometric functions

The ACT sometimes has one question dealing with graphs of trigonometric functions. These usually deal with how parts of the functions change the amplitude and period of the graph. If you have had trigonometry in school these questions should not be too difficult. If you have not had a trigonometry class, just guess and go on to the next question.

Miscellaneous questions

Some questions just require careful reading and thinking.

See: Question 20

Logic Questions

These are perhaps the most obscure questions on the test. They usually will be something along the lines of this:

"If 1 is true, then 2 is true; Which of the following is true?"

For these types of questions, simple reasoning should be applied.

The only answer that makes sense is "If 1 is not true, then 2 is not true", since 2's truth is dependent on 1's truth. Don't let these questions catch you off guard. All they require is a little common sense.

ACT MATH TEST EXPLANATIONS
By **Rajiv Raju**

Please refer to the questions in the Math component of the practice test (**Form 0964E**) in official ACT booklet, Preparing for the ACT .

1)   If we understand absolute value notation, this is a simple case of an expression that needs to be simplified: no application of math concepts.   This is usually the case with the first question on the ACT Math Test.   Just handle each absolute value term in the expression individually.   As you know, either from your previous knowledge or from our introductory section for the Math Test, **any number within an absolute value operator becomes positive, regardless of its sign.**   In the first term, 7-3 = 4, and I4I is 4.   Now move on to the other absolute value term.   3-7 = -4, and I-4I is 4.   If you do not have an understanding of absolute value, there a few tricks you can fall for in this question.   If you did the absolute value operation on each individual number instead of treating the operations within the absolute value as a single term, you would end up with a strange answer.   Using this logic, you would get 4 for the first term, and 10 for the second term.   Subtracting these two numbers would yield -6, or choice B, which is wrong.   You would end up with Choice E if you ignored the absolute value operation and simply treated the expression as (7-3) - (3-7), which would end up equaling 8.   Choice A and C are not trick patterns, but they are wrong nonetheless.   Choice D is the correct answer because if you perform the absolute value operation correctly, we should end up with 4 - 4 =0.

2)   This is a question where we must take a verbal description and put it into equation form to solve the problem posed.   A good initial strategy to tackle these problems is to identify which elements of the problem are constant, and which ones vary.   The two constants in this equation are the flat rate of $30, and the final bill of $210.   The varying element is the $45 per hour charge for the consultants work.   The variable we are solving for is the number of hours the consultant must work.

$45 x (the number of hours) + $30 flat rate = $210 bill

Now put this in full algebraic form, using a letter for the variable (in this case, x)

$$45x + 30 = 210.$$

Now solve the equation for x by subtracting 30 from both sides and dividing both sides by 45. You should end up with x = 4, which is choice G. Beware for the trick answer choice that can be obtained if you set up your equation wrong by putting the $30 in front of the x term and using the $45 as the constant:

$$30x + 45 = 210$$

If you solve this, you would end up with 5.5, or choice J, which is obviously wrong.

3) This question requires us to take the verbal description of the problem and put it in an algebraic form. More specifically, we need to set up two simple equations and compare the resulting answers. We can do this because both equations we set up must be equal to 1008 miles. Now we must chose what our variable will represent. We can do this by identifying which element of the problem is varying. This element is the number of gallons, which is dependent on the number of miles per gallon. So our two equations would be set up like the following:

(14 miles per gallon) x (number of gallons) = 1008 gallons

(36 miles per gallon) x (number of gallons) = 1008 gallons

In full algebraic form, this would be represented as:

$$14x = 1008$$

36x = 1008

Solve for x in both equations and you get x = 72 and x = 28 respectively. However, after solving one of these equations, don't just simply pick answers E and B because they are 72 and 28. We must do the comparison between these values by subtracting 28 from 72, which is 44. Vehicle A needs 44 more gallons than Vehicle B to travel 1008 miles, so choice C is the correct answer.

4) For this question, we simply need to combine like terms to simplify the expression. First, we can eliminate any choices that have terms with powers that are not even in the original expression. Choice G can be eliminated because the t^6 is a higher powered term than is present in the expression. The same can be said for choice H which has the term t^4. Now we can actually start condensing the expression. First we can look at the t^2 terms:

$$t^2 - 82t^2 = -81 \ t^2.$$

Now we can do the t terms:

$$-59t + 60t = t$$

There is only one answer choice that has both of these terms in one expression after doing this condensation: Choice J, or $-81t^2 + t + 54$. We can eliminate choices F and K because they lack either $-81t^2$ or t. These types of questions are extremely easy if you are diligent with making sure you are condensing only like terms.

5) There are three things that we must realize about the figure before we answer the problem: 1) All sides of a square are equal, 2)All sides of an equilateral triangle are equal, 3) The triangle shares one of the 6 inch sides with the square. Knowing this, we can deduce that all the sides of this figure created by the triangle and square have a length of 6 inches. To find the perimeter, we must simply add up the lengths of all of the sides. Since there are 5 sides each with a length of 6 inches, the perimeter of the figure ABCDE is 30 inches, or Choice C. Be wary not to choose choice B, however, as it is easy not to

count the bottom side of the figure that is already labeled with a 6. When you are rushed for time, you may quickly think that you don't need to count that side, and choice B accounts for that incorrect thinking pattern.

6) We must use the "FOIL" technique and subsequently simplify the expression by combining like terms to answer this question. Don't simply think you can multiply 4z with z and 3 with -2. There are two trick answer choices related to this. Choice F is an answer one would probably choose if they did this incorrect process of multiplying out the expression and incorrectly multiplied 3 and -2 to get -5(under timed conditions, this careless mistake is entirely possible!). Choice G is wrong because it is the same wrong answer pattern except with the correct multiplication of 3 and -2. Now we can expand the expression by multiplying the first terms(4z and z), the outer terms(4z and -2), the inner terms(3 and z), and the last terms(3 and -2) to get the following expression:

$$4z^2 - 8z + 3z - 6$$

Combining like terms will yield:

$$4z^2 - 5z - 6$$, or answer choice J.

7) This is another problem where a written description must be translated into an algebraic expression. Since the "given number" is the unknown, we can assign a variable to it. The equation should look like this.

$$4x = 8$$

Solve for x and you get x =20. However, this is not the answer to the question. The final question is what is 15% of this number. Simply do the operation 0.15 x 20 on your calculator and you will get 3.0, which is answer C. A trick answer here is choice A, which you would get if you simply multiplied 8 by 0.15. If you are not reading carefully, you may focus on the statement "given number is 8" and subsequently interpret that this is the number you must find 15% of, which would yield 1.2.

8) This is another algebra question where you must add up all the terms and solve the equation in terms of x. We can do this because it is stated that all of the terms add up to 447. If we combine all the like terms we should get 6x + 3. Now we can set up our equation:

$$6x+3 = 447$$

Solve for x and we should get x = 74, or Choice H. The only way you can go wrong in this question is if you don't add up the numbered terms correctly. Otherwise, this is a very straightforward problem.

9) For this question, we need to apply the midpoint formula to solve an algebraic equation to get the ordered pair we need for the answer. The midpoint of a segment can be found by just finding the average value of the x values and y values, respectively, for both end points.

$$[X_1 + X_2] / 2 \text{ and } [Y_1 + Y_2] / 2$$

Above is midpoint formula for both x and y values. Knowing this, we can set up two algebraic equations to find the coordinates of A by solving for the other x coordinate corresponding to A and the y coordinate corresponding to A:

For X: $(7 + x) / 2 = 5$

For Y: $(3 + y) / 2 = 4$

By solving just solving for x, we can eliminate all of the wrong answer choices because only one choice has x=3 for the x coordinate. Therefore, Choice D is the correct answer.

10) For this question, we can estimate where the dot for point D should be, and we can use process of elimination to arrive at the

correct answer. From knowledge of the properties of rectangles, opposite sides should be equal in length. Look at the difference in the y values between A and B. We can do this by subtracting B's y value, 2, from A's y value, 5, which means that the difference is 3. That means that the increase in y value from point C to point D would be 3 to keep the proportions characteristic of a rectangle. Since point C is at (6, -6), point D would have to have a y value of -3. The only answer choice that has this is Choice F. Also, the x values between points A and B are 4 units apart, so it would make sense that if point C has an x value of 6, point D would have an x value of 10.

11) For this problem, we can use simple arithmetic and some common sense to arrive at the same answer we would get if we used matrix multiplication. All ACT matrix problems can usually be answered with common sense rather than actual matrix operations. The first matrix gives us the number of each type of shirt sold at stores X and Y. The second matrix shows the cost of each type of shirt. To find the total value of the entire inventory, we must simply multiply the number of each type of shirt by their individual costs for both stores.

For store X, the total value of the inventory is found by doing the following operation:

$$(100) \times (\$5) + (200) \times (\$10) + (150) \times (\$15) = \$4750 \text{ total}$$
inventory value for X

For Store Y:

$$(120) \times (\$5) + (50) \times (\$10) + (100) \times (\$15) = \$2600$$

Add these two values together and we get the total value of the inventory to be $7350, or choice E. If we follow this simple procedure, there is no way to end up with the other possible answer choices, which don't seem to fall into any particular trick patterns.

12) This question requires the application of two basic geometric principles: 1) Supplementary angles must add up to 180^0 and 2) All

the angles in a triangle add up to 180^0. To make our calculations easier however, we can recognize that the exterior angle z is equal to the sum of the two given angles in the triangle. Thus, angle z is 129^0. Now we can use the angle supplementary rule to find angles x and y.

For X:

$$180^0 - 57^0 = 123^0$$

For Y:

$$180^0 - 72^0 = 108^0$$

Add all angles x, y, and z together to get 360^0, or Choice J. Be wary for choice G, which has been placed to trick people who only add up angles x and y and neglect z. Also, do not pick choice K just for the sake of it being there. Calmly go through the problem and try to answer it. If you cannot, do not pick K; skip the problem and go back to it if you have time. Pick K only if you can definitively say that there is not enough information to solve the problem. Most of the time, this answer choice ends up being wrong.

13) This is a simple division problem to find what percentage a certain number is of a larger number. Look at the chart under the number of voters section and we can see that 30 people voted for Whitney. What we are being asked to do is simply finding what percentage 30 is of 200. We can do this by dividing 30 by 200, which yields 15%., or choice A. There is absolutely no trick to this question; it is simply just reading the chart properly and doing this single operation. The only way you can err in this problem is picking the wrong number off of the chart.

14) To tackle this problem, we should set up an algebraic proportion to find the number of votes Lue is projected to receive in the election. We know that 80 people out of 200 favored Lue as the mayor, or 40% of the poll. Therefore, we can set up a proportion that looks like this:

$$80/200 = (x/10000)$$

Solving for x, we get x = 4000 people, or choice H.   Again, be careful that you refer to the correct number on the chart when answering this question.   If you accidentally picked 30, which actually corresponds to Whitney, you would end up with 1500, or choice F, as a final answer, which is wrong.

15)   For this question, we must apply the fact that a circle is $360°$ to find the angle of the portion corresponding to the Gomez votes on a circle representing the proportion of voters for each candidate.   First, we must find what percentage of the 200 pollsters voted for Gomez. We can do this by dividing 40 by 200 and we find that 20 % voted for Gomez.   Now we must find the angle on the circle that would represent 20% of the pollsters.   To do this, we simply multiply $360°$ by 0. 2, which yields $72°$ or choice B.   Choices E is present for people who carelessly pick the wrong number from the chart (in this case, 80 which corresponds to Lue).   Choice C also contains the same type of trick, as 90(degrees) corresponds to an angle that would be obtained by using 50 from the chart, which corresponds to Blackcloud.

16)   For this question, we need to use some deduction to find the ratio.   Because point D is the midpoint of segment EC, we can infer that ED and DC are each half of AB.   We also know that triangle ADE has the same height as ADB.   With this information, we can just estimate that the two triangles flanking ADB are together equal to the area of ADB.   Therefore, the ratio of AED to ADB is 1:2, or answer G. We can prove this with the formula for the area of a triangle where the base represents the segment AB and the height represents the height of ADB.

$$(bh)/2 = \text{Area of ADB}$$

Since the segment ED is half of AB, we can represent ED as 0.5b. Substituting this in to the equation would yield (bh)/4.

$$[(bh)/4] / [(bh/2)] \text{ yields a ratio of 1:2.}$$

17)   This is a very straightforward problem if you know the definition of the slope of a parallel line.   The slope of a parallel line has the same slope as the original line.   So a parallel line to y = (2x/3) -4 would also have a slope of 2/3.   Therefore, the correct answer is choice E.   Be wary of choice B, which gives the slope of the line perpendicular to the original line, not parallel.

18) Though we can solve this problem using algebra, we can do this much more easily numerically by working backwards from the answer. A good strategy for answers that list numbers in increasing order is starting with the middle choice.   In this case, we can start with choice H, or 12 feet as the shorter piece.   If two pieces were cut from the 30 foot board, then the other piece would be 18 feet long. Since the problem is asking for the ratio between the two pieces, we would divide 12 by 18.   Luckily, this ends up being a 2:3 ratio, which is what the question is looking for, so we can eliminate all the other answer choices and pick Choice C.   Be wary, however, of choice K, which on may pick if they didn't read carefully and picked the larger piece instead of the shorter piece.

19)   If you use your calculator and know the definition of an integer, this question is extremely easy.   If you plug in √58 into the calculator, you should get approximately 7.6158.   Since an integer is defined as a positive whole number, the smallest integer greater than this number would be 8, or choice C.   Even if you did not have a calculator (which you absolutely should have!), you should know that the nearest whole number square root is 8, and that this √64.   So we can eliminate choices D and E.   Since the question is asking for the value of the smallest integer greater than sq root of 58, we can eliminate A and B because we know that these values are less than the √58 because √49 is 7 and √16 is 4.

20)   For this problem, we must find the total surface area of the area that needs to be painted on the walls to determine how many cans of paint are needed for the job.   Since the walls are rectangular, the area of each wall would be the length times the height:

10 x 15= 150 ft sq.

Since all the walls are the same size, we can multiply this value by 4 to get the total surface area of the 4 walls, which is 600 ft squared. However, we need to subtract the areas of the door and the window, which do not need to be painted. The area of the rectangular window is 15 ft sq and the area of the rectangular door is 24.5 ft sq. Subtract both of these from 600 ft sq and we get 560.5 ft sq that needs to be painted. Now we need to look at how many feet each gallon of paint covers. The lowest amount that one gallon can cover is 300 ft sq, so we would need 2 paint cans for the job, which is choice G. Be sure not to simply multiply 4 by 300 sq ft, assuming that each wall is 300 sq feet and that you would need 4 gallons of paint. Be sure to read all the information in this problem and it is hard to get tricked.

21)   The simplest way to answer this problem is to put the equation into a factorable form and confirm and choose the correct set of answers (assuming you are comfortable with the process of factoring). To put the equation into factorable form, subtract 8 from each side of the equation so we end up with:

$$X^2 + 2x - 8 = 0$$

To factor, we must realize that the x^2 term is factored into two "x" terms, and that because there are terms after this x^2, we should end up with a factorization in the form of:

$(x + y) (x + z) = 0$; where y and z represent constants.

To find which constants are correct, we need to think about which combination of numbers can be multiplied together to get -8 and can be added together to get 2(so that when we "FOIL" the expression, we should get our original equation). The two numbers that have this property are 4 and -2. (4 x -2 = -8 ; 4+ (-2) = 2) So our y and z values are 4 and -2. Our expression should look like the following:

$(x+4) (x-2) = 0$

Solving for x in each term yields x= -4 and x = 2, which are the two numbers listed in choice A. Don't fall for picking choice C which lists the numbers that are present in the factored expression before we solve for x. If you cannot factor quickly enough, there is another way to approach this problem, using the graphing capabilities of a graphing calculator. Doing this, we can find when the graph intersects the x axis to find the solutions to the equation.

22) We need to know some properties of exponents in order to find this problem. Plugging in values for a is too cumbersome; simplify the expression find the answer. We know that exponents with the same base can be condensed in an expression. In this case, one exponentiated term is being divided by another exponentiated term with the same base. When this operation is done, the exponent of the term under the divisor is subtracted from the exponent of the term above the divisor. In this case, we would subtract 4 from 6.and the 3's would be canceled out because 3 is being divided by 3:

$$(3a^4) / (3a^6) = a^{-2}$$

The expression a^{-2} is equivalent to $1/(a^2)$, which is answer choice K. If you neglect the fact that 4 -6 = -2 when condensing the expression(which is possible when you are dealing with exponents and you are in a time crunch), you would end up with choice H. Also, don't mistakenly rewrite a^{-2} as $-(1/(a^2))$, or answer choice J.

23) The only knowledge that is required for this question is a very basic knowledge of the coordinate axis system. We must note that the intersection of the x and y axis indicates a point of (0,0), and that values higher than this point have a positive y value, while points lower than this point have a negative y value. Points to the right of this point have a positive x value, and points to the left of this point have a negative x value. Knowing this, we can find the quadrant(s) that have x and y values with opposite signs. Choice A is wrong because both the x and y values would be positive in this quadrant, as points in this quadrant are higher and to the right of (0,0). We can also eliminate choice C and D because these include quadrant I as a correct choice. Choice B is wrong because both x and y are negative in this quadrant because all points here are lower than and to the left of (0,0). Choice E is the correct answer because quadrant II and quadrant IV both have x and y values that have opposite signs from each other. In quadrant II, the x values are negative while the y

values are positive. In quadrant IV, the x values are positive while the y values are negative.

24) This problem is similar to problem 2 but easier in that we don't need to actually solve the equation we set up. Because $5.25 is the cost of making each basketball, this number should be the coefficient of the variable b in the problem. The fixed cost is the constant, and since we are finding the total cost of producing b basketballs, we simply add $1,400 to the expression. Our final result should look like the following:

$5.25b + $1,400, or answer choice K.

There are a few trick answer choices in this problem. Choice H mixes up the constant number with the variable number so that the $1,400 is in front of b, which is incorrect. In choice F, $5.25 is simply added to $1,400, and $1,405.25 is the term in front of b, which is not the correct coefficient. Choice G is wrong because since we are trying to determine the cost of the basketball production, the fixed cost of $1,400 should be added to the expression.

25) Because the two triangles are similar, we can use their proportionality to find the other sides of ABC and ultimately its perimeter. We can set up the following proportion to find side AB by comparing the similar sides of the triangles:

7.5 / 12.5 = 3 / (AB)

Solving for AB yields 5. We can now set up another proportion to find side BC:

(7.5 / 15) = 3 / (BC)

Solving for BC yields 6. Now that we know all the sides we can find the perimeter of the triangle, which is 14 centimeters, or choice B. Don't read the question wrong and calculate the perimeter of MLK, which would yield 35 centimeters, or choice D.

26)   If we know a simple property of root multiplication, we can easily arrive at the answer to this question.   Notice that the only difference between the expression on the right of the equal sign and the number on the left is the a in the denominator.   What would "a" have to be to make a x √7 = 7?   Note that if we multiply a root by the same root, the root signs cancel out and we are left with the number within the root.   Therefore, we would need to multiply √7 by √7 to obtain 7, so "a" = √7, or answer choice G.   Do not waste time solving for "a" algebraically.   The only way you can go wrong in this problem is if you do not know this property of roots.

27) Set up two equations and set them equal to each other to solve this problem.   For the falling balloon, the constant is the balloon's initial altitude, and its altitude varies by 6 m per second.   Therefore we can set up this expression, using a variable representing time:

70m - (6m/s)t

For the rising balloon, the initial altitude is again the constant, and the height is varying by 15 m per second.   We would add the term with 15m/s because this balloon is rising (obviously meaning the altitude is increasing).   The expression should look like this:

10m + (15m/s)t

To find how much time it will take for the two balloons to meet each other, we need to set these expressions equal to one another and solve:

70m - (6m/s)t = 10m + (15m/s)t

Solving for t yields t = 2.857, which rounded off to the nearest tenth, is 2.9, or choice C.   If you set up the equation wrong, adding the (6m/s)t term to 70m, you would end up with t = 6.7, or answer choice B, which is incorrect.   Other than that, this is a straightforward problem.

28) This is a problem that can be solved using a concept called the "counting principle". This principle states that to find the total number of possible results (in this case, routes), you must multiply the number of possibilities for each element (in this case, the roads, the paths, and trails). If you counted out every possibility each with one road, one path, and one trail, you would get the same result. There are four possible roads, two possible bike paths, and six possible hiking trails. According to the counting principle, all we have to do is multiply all these elements:

4 roads x 2 bicycle paths x 6 hiking trails = 48 possibilities, or choice J

The only way of solving this problem is using the counting principle. Choice G is present to trick people who would not use the counting principle and would simply add up the 4 possible roads, 2 possible biking paths, and 6 possible hiking trails to get 12.

29) If we simply know the formula for the volume of a cube, this problem is extremely easy. If the question is asking us the volume of a cube that has edge lengths two inches more than a 2 inch edge length on another cube, then it is obviously asking us the volume of a cube with edge lengths of 4 inches. The formula for the volume of a cube is the edge length cubed or $V=S^3$. However, for people that do not read the question carefully, there are a few trap answers. Choice C is a trick because that is the answer one would arrive at if they simply found the area of one of the sides of the cube, or the area of a square, which is not what the problem is asking us to do. Choice B is also a trick for people who do not read that they must be finding the volume of Cube B rather than Cube A. 8 is the volume of Cube A, not cube B. Similarly to choice C, choice A is wrong because it gives the answer that one would arrive at if they simply found the surface area of one of the sides of cube A, which would be 4. Choice E is correct because it correctly states that the volume of Cube B is 4 x 4.x 4, or 64 inches^3.

30) This is a simple "plug and chug" problem, meaning we simply have to plug in given values into the formula to find the correct answer. For A, we would plug in our initial investment of $10,000. For r, we would plug in 0.04 for the rate of interest. For N, we would

plug in 5 because since the interest is compounded annually, there would be 5 compounding periods within 5 years. Calculating this out, we get $12, 167, which is answer choice B. Be wary of answer choice K, which you would end up with if you plugged in 0.4 for r instead of 0.04. Also, don't fall for choice F, which one may end up picking if they plugged in 1 for n instead of 5, seeing the phrase "compounded annually" and assuming that must mean that n = 1, when in reality n represents the number of compounding within a certain time period.

31)   Because the test makers give us the formula for the surface area of a cylinder, this is another problem where we only need to plug in values to obtain an answer. We can see that the height of the cylinder is 20 centimeters, and the diameter of the cylinder is 20 centimeters. This means that the radius of the cylinder is 10 centimeters. Now we can plug the values into the formula:

$$2\pi (10)^2 + 2\pi (10)(20) = 600\pi, \text{ or choice D}$$

Choice E is a trap for people who don't realize that 20 centimeters is the diameter of the cylinder and not the radius. If you plugged in 20 cm for the radius, you would end up with 1600π.

32)   For this problem, you need an understanding of function notation.   That is, when we are given f(x) and g(x), and we are asked to find f(g(x)), that means that we must plug in g(x) into the variables of f(x). Following this rule and plugging in g(x) into f(x), we should get the following expression:

$$4(x^3 - 2) + 1.$$

Simplifying this, we should get:

$4x^2 -7$, or answer choice H.

Don't fall for answer choice K, which you would obtain if you did the operation g(f(x)) as opposed to f(g(x)).

33)   Since we are given the total number of games, all we must do for this problem is add up the total number of goals scored in all of the games and divide this number by 43 games to get the average number of goals scored per game.   We can find the total number of games by doing this operation:

$$0(4) + (1)(10) + (2)(5) + (3)(9) + (4)(7) + (5)(5) + (6)(1) + (7)(2) = 120.$$

To find the average, we divide 120 by 43, and get 2.790, which rounded to the nearest tenth, is 2.8, or answer choice B.   Be on the look out for the trick answer choices in this problem. Choice A is a trick because you would obtain that answer if you simply added up the numbers on the right hand side of the chart and took the average of that set.   This is obviously not the total number of points, only the different number of points earned each game.   Choice C is also an answer you could end up with if you rounded carelessly.   The question does not ask us to round to the nearest ones place, but the nearest tenth.   2.79 rounds to 2.8 to the nearest tenth, not to 3.0.

34)   For this question we need to know the properties of angles created by a line intersecting two parallel lines, as well as the definition of a supplementary angle, which is an angle that can be added to another angle to add up to 180^0.   From angles created by intersecting lines, the angles transverse from each other(ex angles 1 and 2) are equal.   Since angle 1 is supplementary to x, we must find all the angles that are equal to angle 1.   Because two parallel lines intersected by a third line will have the same sized angles at each intersection point, we can find the angles that are equal to angle 1 at the other intersection point.   At the first intersection point, angle 2 is equal to angle 1.   This means that angle 9 must be equal to angle 10. Since the other line is approaching the parallel lines at a different angle, none of the angles formed by those intersections would be the same as the ones formed by the other intersecting line.   Therefore, the correct answer is choice H because this set has the correct angles.

35)   This is a simple application of exponential rules.   Since every term in the parentheses is being multiplied, we can just exponentiate every term. 3^3 is 27, and $(x^3)^3$ is x^9.   Therefore, the final expression should be $27x^9$, or choice E.   Of course, there are going to be trick

answers waiting for people who are not comfortable with exponent rules. Choices B and C are wrong because when you exponentiate a constant, you don't simply multiply it by the exponent, as is done in these answer choices. Choice D is wrong because when you exponentiate a term that is represented in exponent form, you multiply the exponent that the term is being raised to by the exponent on the term, not add the two numbers, as has been done in choice D.

36) With the addition of a few stipulations, solving inequalities is done in the same manner as solving equations. Like an equation, we must end up with the variable on one side, and the constant on the other. Subtract 4x from each side, and subtract 16 from each side, and you should end up with this expression:

$-24 > 4x$, which solved is $x < -6$, or answer choice F.

One thing that you should remember about inequalities is that if you divide each side by a negative number, the sign changes a direction. This is the only case where it does so, so any choices where the sign changes direction is a trick.

37) This problem does not require any complicated and tedious math. Rather, all we have to know is what quadrant the point P will end up in when we rotate the axis clockwise. Since the circle occupies 4 quadrants, and a 90^0 rotation is ¼th of the circles angle measure, we can assume that the point will end up in the next quadrant with regards to the direction it is rotated in. Since we are rotating clockwise and point P is located in quadrant 1, we should expect that the point will be in quadrant 4 when rotated 90 degrees because quadrant 4 is clockwise from quadrant 1. The only ordered pair of that is in quadrant 4 is choice C, or (5, -1).

38) This is a two step problem. We must first find the missing side of triangle, and use this side to find the sin of angle K. Since this is a right triangle, we can use the Pythagorean Theorem to solve for the missing side:

$$10^2 + x^2 = 12^2$$

Solve for x and you should get x = $\sqrt{44}$. Now you can find sin of angle K because we have all the sides of the triangle. The definition of sin with respect to an angle on a right triangle is the side opposite of the angle/hypotenuse. Therefore, the sin of angle K is $\sqrt{44}$ / 12, or choice K. If you don't know this property, there are several choices to trick you. Choice F is the cos of angle K. Choice G is just the reciprocal of this. Choice J is the cot of angle K, or the reciprocal of tan of angle K. Choice H is the tan of angle K.

39) For this question, we must understand that that the angles on a line must all add up to 180 ^{0}. Also, we must note that angles DBA and EBC are equivalent because they both bisect angles of the same measure and they share the point. Because of the supplementary angle property, the three angles comprising segment AC must add up to 180 ^{0}, and because DBA and EBC are equal and the segment is broken into 3 pieces, all of the angles must be equal to 60^0 because 180 ^{0} divided by 3 is 60^0. Therefore, angle DBE is 60^0, or choice B. This certainly is not a straightforward problem, and it may be a good idea to skip it and move on if you are spending too much time on it.

40) Don't let the scientific notation of the numbers keep you from seeing this as a very simple average problem. Since the question is asking for the average number of hydrogen molecules per cubic centimeter, we simply divide the total number of hydrogen molecules by the total number of cubic centimeters. You can then plug this into your calculator to get 200000000, or 2 x 10^8, which is choice H. If you don't want to plug this expression into your calculator, the division required for this is quite simple. 8 / 4 = 2 and 10^{12} / 10^4 = 10^8. We can split up these operations because the terms are being multiplied, and you would end up with the same result, 2^8. Choice F is the answer you would get if you divided 4 x 10^4 by 8 x 10^{12}, which would give you the average number of cubic centimeters per hydrogen molecule! Choice K is also a trick because it is the answer choice one would pick if they multiplied the number of hydrogen molecules by the number of centimeters.

41) Though this problem may require you to use the intimidating law of cosines, this is a simple case of plugging in given values to obtain a

solution. First we need to define a, b, and c. It would be reasonable to assign the side created by the path of ship A to variable a. The same goes for variable b, which represents the path created by ship B. Side c is the unknown distance between the two ships, and the angle across from side C is angle C. We now need to deduce the value of angle C, and we can do this by looking at the difference between the bearings of ship A and ship B. Because their bearings are measured from the same starting point, we simply have to subtract the lower angled bearing from the higher angled bearing to find angle C in the triangle. The higher bearing, 300^0, starts from the north arrow and ends at side B. The lower bearing, 170^0 degrees, also starts at the north arrow but ends at side A. $300 - 170 = 130^0$, which is the measure of angle C in the triangle. Now we have all the information we need to plug into the formula. Fortunately for us, the question is simply asking us to set up the expression and not to simplify it. Plugging in 30 for side b, 20 for side a, and 130 for angle C. we should end up with the following:

$$c^2 = 20^2 + 30^2 - 2(20)(30)\cos(130).$$

Now take the square root of both sides to solve for C:

$$C = \sqrt{[20^2 + 30^2 - 2(20)(30)\cos(130)]}$$, which happens to be answer choice B. Beware of some trick answer choices. Choice C just has the bearing of ship A for angle C, and Choice D just has the bearing of ship B for angle C. Choice E just has an angle where the two bearings are added.

42) Before you look at the answer choices in this problem, first find the decimal values of the two fractions 1/5 and 1/3, which are .2 and .333 repeating. Immediately, you can eliminate choices F, H, and K because choice F is bigger than this range, choice H is smaller than this range, and choice K is bigger than this range. Now you can solve this problem simply by seeing if the difference between 1/3 and the rational number in the answer choice is equal to the difference between the rational number and 1/5. This is not the case for choice G, but is for choice J, or 4/15.

43) To do this problem, we must realize that angles ADC and BCD as well as sides AD and BC are equivalent from the definition of the

isosceles trapezoid. SAS(side-angle-side) makes triangles ACD and BDC congruent and allows us to conclude that angle ACD is 25 and that angle BCD=35 + angle ACD =60. We now know two of the three angles of triangle BCD. Therefore angle DBC=180-60-25=95^0 or choice B. If you had trouble coming up with all the reasons for the correct answer given here, just make a guess based on intuition and estimation from the picture. On the ACT you never need to prove anything. You just need to come up with the right answer.

44) The easiest way to answer this problem is to first find out what one side of the smaller square is, and try out different answer choices added to that side length to see if that value squared is 50 square centimeters. As with all problems where you try different answer choices and the answer choices are going in ascending order, start with the middle choice. First, to find the side length of the smaller square, we should take the $\sqrt{18}$. Now we can try different answer choices added to $\sqrt{18}$ to see if the side length is correct. Start with $4\sqrt{2}$ since it is the middle choice:

$[4\sqrt{2} + \sqrt{18}]^2 = 98$, which is larger than 50. We can eliminate choices J and K because they are larger than this. Now try the next lowest choice, $2\sqrt{2}$:

$[2\sqrt{2} + \sqrt{18}]^2 = 50$ cm squared, which is the correct answer choice G. Often, using elimination techniques such as these is much easier than solving the problem algebraically.

45) This question is easy if we know some basic square roots and the definition of a rational number. A rational number is a number that can be simplified as a fraction. Choice A is wrong because the 2 is not a perfect square and does not have a rational answer. Choice B, C, and D are wrong for the same reason. Choice E can be square rooted into the fraction 8/7, so it is a rational number and the correct answer.

46) For this question, we must analyze what is happening a and b in the expression. Because a is less than b, the absolute value of the (a-b) would be the equivalent to (b-a), because absolute value is an indicator of the numerical distance between two numbers. Now we must find the expression that is equal to b-a. Choice K, or -(a-b) is equal to b-a when the expression is simplified. Choice F is a trick

answer for people who assume that a is a negative number because they see a < b. Just because a < b does not mean that it is a negative number. If you assume that a is a negative number, you will get a negative number that will become (a+b) when its absolute value is found.

47) This is a question where you have to use the principle of averages and solve an algebraic equation. First, we should calculate the total number of points that Tom has now by multiplying 78 by 5, which yields 390. Because there are six elements in the set we are taking the average of we can set up this expression:

(390+x) / 6 =80; where x represents the test score that Tom needs to have an 80 average. Solve for x and we get x = 90, or answer choice A. Surprisingly, there are no trick answer choices in this question; if you know how to answer the problem, there are not many places where you can go wrong.

48) In this problem, we must realize that the sign of the x and y values is irrelevant because the values are squared within the square root sign. We must also note that this problem does not require us to do any operations in the complex domain. We must therefore look for the point which has the highest magnitude of x and y in the real domain. Magnitude disregards sign and measures the distance of the value from the origin. With this in mind, we can now eliminate answer choices. Choice K is wrong because though this point has a large x magnitude, it does not have a y value with enough magnitude to have the highest modulus. Choice G, H, and J are wrong for the same reasons. Choice F is correct because this point has both the highest x magnitude and the highest y magnitude of any point on the graph, and this would translate to the largest modulus value.

49) The easiest way to solve this problem is to express the 8 and 4 on each side as powers of 2. Doing this will put the equation in this form:

$$2^{(3(2x+1))} = 2^{(2(1-x))}$$

Because we have the equation in a form where the bases of the exponential terms are the same, we can cancel out the bases(technically by taking log base 2 of each side), and we are left with a simple algebraic expression:

6x+3 = 2-2x; solving for x yields -1/8, or answer choice C.

Be careful in your extension of the terms in the exponent, or you can fall into some trick answer patterns. For example, you would get choice B if you extended out the right exponent and got 2x instead of - 2x. You could also get choice E, or 1/7, if you incorrectly expressed the 8 and 4 as powers of 2. In this case you could mix up the exponents on each yielding $2^{(2(3x+1))} = 2^{(2(1-x))}$, which solved would yield 1/7 for x.

50) For this question, we simply need to know the definitions of an even and odd function. An even function is a function that has a mirror image across the y axis. An odd function is a function that has a mirror image across the origin. In this question, we are fortunately given the formal definitions of even and odd, but we can just look at the graph to arrive at the correct answer. Checking to see if the graph is an even function, we can see that if an x value yields a particular y value, the -x value yields the same y value, indicating symmetry across the y axis. This satisfies the definition of an even function, so choice F is the correct answer. We can see that the function is not odd because there is no symmetry across the origin, and for a particular x value, f(-x) is not equal to -f(x). Choices H, J, and K are also incorrect answer choices because the function is even, it is not even close to the graph of the inverse cotangent function, and it is clearly defined at π because the domain stretches from around -6 to 6, which includes π.

51) This is an involved problem that requires us to keep careful track of a large set of numbers. A good way to solve problems such as these is to think about the problem in units. For example, since the problem is asking us for all the numbers between 100 and 999 that satisfy the conditions set forth, we can look at 100-200 first to see how many numbers satisfy the condition in there. We can then multiply this number by the number of "hundred ranges" there are (ex. 200-300, 300-400, etc.). For any number in the range from 100-999, only

the units and tens places can have a 0. First, let's list out all of the possible values for units where a 0 is present in the tens digit, focusing on the 100-200 range:

100, 101, 102, 103, 104, 105, 106, 107, 108, 109.

This is a set of 10 numbers. Now let's look at the possible tens place numbers with a 0 in the units place:

110, 120, 130, 140, 150, 160, 170, 180, 190.

This is a set of 9 numbers. The 19 numbers listed are the only numbers with at least one 0 digit in the number. The tens and units digits shown above are the only ones that have this property in the 200-300, 300-400, 400-500, 500-600, 600-700, 700-800, 800-900, and 900-1000 range. Since there are 9 of these "ranges", and 19 combinations of tens and units digits that satisfy the conditions in each range, we can multiply 19 by 9 to get our 171. Since the problem is asking for a probability, we would divide this number by 900, giving us a final answer of 171/900, or choice D. Notice how we don't use 899 because the problem mentions that the values are inclusive, so we must include 100 in our probability calculation. Don't fall for answer choice A, which puts the combinations of tens and units digits for each "hundred range" over 900, as this is not the correct probability.

52) What can slope be considered as? It makes sense that the absolute value slope can also be defined as the angle at which a line is traveling, on top of the definition that it is a measure of the rate of change of a line. Since angles a and b have the same slope, we can infer that lines q and r have the same magnitude of slope, regardless of their signs, since they are approaching the x axis and beyond at the same angle. Since q has a positive slope, r must have a negative slope of the same magnitude. We can find the slope of line q by placing it in slope-intercept form:

Y= 2x+1; the negative form of this slope is -2, which is answer choice F. Don't pick choice J, as the lines would have to be parallel for them both to have the same slope. Also, don't pick choice K ever unless you have a definitive reason why there is not enough information to solve the problem, as opposed to just picking it because you cannot figure out how to solve the problem.

53) In this problem, we must understand that inverse tangent(a/b) is an angle value. Since this angle is represented by this expression, this would be the angle that is across from side a and adjacent to side b. Now we must find the expression that expresses cosine of this angle. As we know, cosine on a right triangle is defined as the adjacent side / hypotenuse. So the cosine of the angle would be represented as $b/(\sqrt{(a^2+b^2)})$, or choice D. Choice C represents sine of this angle, choice E represents csc of this angle, choice B represents cotangent of this angle, and choice A represents tangent of this angle.

54) This question is simply asking us to find the area of the circle that models the situation in the description. The area of a circle is $\pi(radius)^2$. In this problem, the radius is 52 miles, so we can plug this in for radius. Performing the operation gives us around 8,494 miles, which is closest to 8,500 miles, or choice J, Be wary of choice G, which you would obtain if you simply took the square of 52 without multiplying this value by π.

55) If you know the standard form of a circle, this problem is a direct application of that principle. Since the circle is centered around the origin, the left of the equation would just be $x^2 + y^2$. Since the radius is 52 mi, the right of the equation should look like 52^2. The final equation should look like this:

$$X^2 + y^2 = 52^2,$$ or answer choice E.

Don't fall for trick answers like A, B and D which don't square the radius. Also, you should know that $(x+y)^2$ is not $=$ to x^2+y^2, which is why choice C is wrong.

56) If you draw a picture, this problem becomes much easier. Remember, when ever possible, you should always write your thinking down on paper to free up precious space in your short term memory. First, draw out a circle representing the range of the

WGGW signal, which would be a circle with a radius of 52 miles. Now draw a point representing WGWB 100 miles away from WGGW (any direction is fine, but left or right is preferred as it makes visualizing the problem easier). Draw the area that represents the range of this station. This is a circle with a radius of 60 miles. If you have drawn the circles correctly, you should see that the circles overlap within the 100 miles separating the stations. How do we find the range where the circles overlap? To do this, we simply add the two radii and see how much greater this sum is than 100 miles, as any mile over 100 is an area where the circles must be overlapping. 52 + 60 = 112, which is 12 more miles than 100, so the correct answer is choice G. There are several trick answer choices in this problem. Choice F is a trick because it is simply a subtraction of the smaller radius from the larger radius. This would be the area of overlap if the two stations were 104 miles apart. Choice H is also a trick because it is simply a subtraction of the radius of 60 from the distance between the stations. Choice K is wrong similarly because it is just a subtraction of the radius of 52 from the distance between the two stations.

57) Solving this problem algebraically would take much more time than you can spare on the mathematics section. Fortunately for us, the ACT gives us a graph of the two equations so we can do a graphical analysis to find the correct solution to the inequality $(x-1)^4 < (x-1)$. We can do this simply by seeing where the graph of x-1 has a larger y value than the graph of $(x-1)^4$. The only place where this occurs is from 1<x<2, the end points of this range being the intersection points of the two graphs. Therefore, choice E is the correct answer. Beware of choice C, which may seem right at first glance, but in reality has an incorrect range for the solutions for the inequality. For x<1, $(x-1)^4$ is clearly larger than x-1, and the same is true for x>2,

58) The simplest way to do this problem is to use an example number fitting the criteria given in the problem and seeing which expression yields a result equal to x-y. Obviously, we do not want to pick a number that has the same tens and units digits as this type of number will have certain properties not common to other two digit numbers. We must pick a two digit number that has distinct values for u and t. To make our calculations simple, let's pick 21. Plug this number into the formulas in the answer choices systematically until you find one that works. First we try F:

9(2-1) = 9 x=21 and y =12.   21-12= 9.

So choice F works for this example. To make sure that this applies to all numbers fitting this criteria, we should try one more number, 52, for instance:

9(5-2)= 27 x=52 and y = 25.   52-25 = 27.

We can be fairly certain that choice F is the correct expression that is equal to x-y. To show that the other choices are wrong, we can plug one of these numbers in to see if we get a wrong answer. If we use t=2 and u=1 on choice G, we would end up with -9, which is not equal to 21-12, which is 9.   If we do this for choice H, we would get 17, which is not equal to this subtraction either.   Choice J would yield 7 for t=2 and u=1, which is wrong.   Choice K only works for two digit numbers which have the same T and U values of 0.

59) For this question, we do not need to use the distance formula to find the height of the triangle to find its area. Because the coordinates are given, we can just look at the y values of these coordinates to see what the y displacement, or height of the triangle is. The base of the triangle has is present at y =3. The top point of the triangle, point A, is present at y = 5. Therefore, we can see that the height of the triangle is 2 units. For the base of the triangle, we can measure the difference between the x coordinates of the two points that define this side of the triangle to find the length of this side. Point C has an x coordinate of 1, and point B has an x coordinate of 5, so the length of the base is 4 units. The formula for the area of a triangle is bh / 2. Plug the values for the height and base into the formula to get the answer:

(4)(2) / 2 = 4, or choice A.

Don't get tricked into picking choice D, which you would arrive at if you simply multiplied the base length and the height and did not divide by 2.

60)   To do this problem, we must find the first term of the series, or a, so we can easily find the second term by multiplying a by the common ratio of 0.15.   We are given the formula for the sum of an infinite geometric series which we can use to find a.   Since the sum of the series is 200, and r is 0 .15, we can solve the equation for a:

$$200 = a / (1- 0.15) \text{ ; solving for a gives us a } = 170.$$

Being tricky as usual, the ACT math section gives us choice J, which is not the answer to the question.   It is crucial to note that 170 is the first term of the sequence, not the second term.   To find the second term, we must multiply 170 by .15, which gives us 25.5, or choice F.

READING STRATEGY
By **Rajiv Raju**

Key Reading Strategies

*-**Do not dwell on the passage.** Your objective is not to memorize the passage on the first pass. You want to just learn what the passage is generally about and where the details are located so that you can find them after you read the questions. You will have to refer back to the passage, so you can not afford to spend too much time on the first reading.*

*-**Adjust your reading speed to the importance of the content you are reading.** If the author's purpose and perspective in the passage are being discussed, you should read through this part of the passage slowly and carefully. When dealing with the supporting details and examples within a passage, you should significantly increase your reading speed.*

*-**It is more important to carefully read the questions than to carefully read the entire passage.** Remember that your score is only dependent on the number of correct answers, and not on how well you understand the passage. It is possible to understand the passage very well and still get many questions wrong if you do not read the questions carefully or spend enough time on them.*

*-**The reason for the correct answer is always explicitly stated in the passage.** If you can not find a reason for picking an answer in the passage, then do not pick it as the correct answer. You must almost always go back to find proof that your answer is correct.*

*-**There are no hidden meanings** in the passages, No deep interptation is ever needed. There is only one correct answer and the reason for it is always in the passage.*

*-**Don't waste time marking up the passage.** If you do write on the passage, limit this to a few underlined statements. Do not take notes*

on the passage, as this will waste much of the precious time that can be used for reading the questions carefully.

The ACT Reading section tests your reading skill and speed. You will have to read the entire passage and understand it. Many of the questions can only be answered by going back to the passage and looking for evidence to support the answer. **The passage always has the information to answer the question, but it may take time to find the information.** Many students will not be able to finish the reading test in the allotted 35 minutes. If you have difficulty finishing this section, you might consider carefully reading three of the four passages and guessing on the fourth passage. Assuming that you are able to correctly answer all of the questions in three of the passages and assuming you get three of the ten questions correct on the fourth passage just from the laws of probability, you will have a raw score of 33 which corresponds to a scaled score of 29 based on the scoring chart in **Preparing for the ACT**. This may be a better score than what you might get if you rushed through all four of the passages without fully understanding them.

Here is the suggested strategy. Read the entire passage-almost skim- as quickly as you can **without dwelling on all the details**. You should however **be aware of where the details are located so you can quickly find them when you answer questions**. When you answer the questions, you should always go back to the passage to find evidence to support the correct answer. There may be a few general questions about the theme or tone of entire passage that may not require you to go back to the passage, but **you should be going back to passage for most of the questions.** When you answer the questions keep in mind that **there is only one correct answer and the reason for the answer is always in the passage.** No outside knowledge is needed and even the reasoning questions only require simple direct inference. **If you can not find a specific reason in the passage to support an answer choice, then do not pick it as the correct answer.** If you find any evidence for why an answer choice is wrong, eliminate the choice from consideration. **Do not think that an answer is correct for some reason that you do not see.** This is time consuming but will increase your accuracy substantially. In your English class you may have been expected to interpret literature to find hidden meanings. These "hidden meanings" might be debatable. This is not a problem in English class since you can write a response to defend a debatable interpretation. This kind of "deep interpretation" can get you in trouble on the ACT reading section. The ACT can never test you on debatable hidden meanings, since there can only be one right answer on a multiple choice test. **Never look for "hidden meaning" on the ACT reading test, just look at what is explicitly stated and keep interpretation to a minimum.**

Almost all ACT Reading Section questions can be categorized into 4 question types:

Rhetorical Analysis Questions

Direct Citation Questions

General Passage Questions

"Odd Man Out" Questions

RHETORICAL ANALYSIS QUESTIONS

These are questions that usually ask the function of a particular paragraph or sentence in the context of the passage. These are somewhat more difficult than other questions because you must often think about what the best description of the information given is. Sometimes, a rhetorical analysis question will ask you about some figurative language used in the passage, and ask what this language represents, as in question 4. Most of the time, however, you can use some common sense to figure out how all the information in the described lines can be described under one purpose. For example, in question 24, the question asks us the main function of paragraph 2. If you read the paragraph, you can see that most of the information relates to the milestones in Armstrong's career. We can therefore infer that the purpose of the second paragraph is to list events that helped Armstrong's career, which is essentially choice G.

DIRECT CITATION QUESTIONS

These questions entail exactly what the category suggests. You must look for specific information directly stated in the passage to answer these questions. There are two variations of these questions. The easier variation is the question type that gives you the actual lines where you need to look for the information. An example of this is question 15, where specific lines are given in the question to refer to. A harder variety of the direct citation question is the question that does not mention specific lines to refer to. Rather, you must find the answer to the question by knowing the general area where to look for the information. While this may be an intimidating task, there is a process that you can go through that, with time, will allow you to answer questions of this second variety much easier. This can be done by looking for key words in the question and answer choices and subsequently finding that concentration of words within the passage in close proximity. Once you find this concentration of words, you should determine the context of those words, and if the context of these words is correct, the answer choice is almost always correct. An example of a question which can be answered with this technique is question 18. In this case, we can see that the words "interactions", "complex" and the phrase "not yet well understood", are all in close proximity and are in correct context within the passage, so we can infer that choice G is correct.

GENERAL PASSAGE QUESTIONS

These are questions that simply require a knowledge of the key ideas in the passage, and can only be easily answered with a skim of the passage or information gathered from other questions. In some cases, the general passage question types are some of the first questions after the passage. Usually quickly skimming through the passage will provide sufficient information to answer these questions, but if you are uncomfortable with this, you can skip these initial questions and answer them once you have gotten more information about the passage from answering the later questions. As stated earlier in this section, skimming should just involve quickly finding the main ideas of the passage without focusing on the minute details and intricacies of the passage, though a general knowledge of the structure of the passage will help with later questions that require you to quickly identify details. An example of one of these question patterns is question 1. Even a rudimentary skim would tell us that the structure of the passage is of a narrator dictating her impressions of another person based on their conversations, as this is how the entire passage is structured.

"ODD MAN OUT" QUESTIONS

This is a very common question type on the ACT Reading Section. In these types, you need to find the answer choice that is incorrect. Basically, this is the reverse of a direct citation question in that you need to look out for the answer choice that isn't supported by the passage. The easiest way to do this is to show that the other answer choices are supported by the passage. An example of this is question 17, where you must show which answer choice is the only one not characterized as a cause of food crises during the "Little Ice Age."

If you can finish the test with this approach you should do very well. Even if you are unable to finish the test, you may still be able to get a respectable score if you do well on the portion of the test that you do complete. Remember to fill in all the answer choices for the questions that you did not have time for. You have a 25% chance of getting these questions right, as the reading section has four answer choices per question.

The next chapter goes through all 40 questions in the reading section of the booklet and illustrates how, in each case, the information in the passage supports the one correct answer and often contradicts the incorrect answer choices.

ACT READING EXPLANATIONS
By **Rajiv Raju**

Please refer to the questions in the Reading component of the practice test (**Form 0964E**) in official ACT booklet, Preparing for the ACT .

Passage 1:

1) If you are to attack this question, you should have done at least a quick skim of the passage before looking at the questions. When a question asks about structure, it is essentially asking for the most generalized summary that can be reasonably associated with the passage. A minute's glance at the passage can reveal a great deal about its core layout. If you have even read the first sentence, you would immediately know that Choice A is incorrect. It is clearly stated in the first sentence of the passage that the woman that the narrator is referring to does not dream at all, so it is impossible for the narrator and her to share their dreams in equal detail. Choice C is easily spotted as incorrect even with a rudimentary understanding of the details of the passage, as it is clear that the narrator is speaking from a first person perspective, as opposed to a third person perspective where the narrator is disconnected from the immediate actions of the people described in the passage, as is indicated in this choice. Choice D is incorrect because the narrator only mentions the specifics of her dreams and the woman's reactions starting with the ninth paragraph. Choice B is correct because it accurately describes the happenings in the passage: the narrator musing about a woman who cannot dream, basing her understanding of this woman off of her conversations with her about dreams.

2)   This is a question where the technique of looking for key words related to the answer choices is helpful. In this case, the question is practically set up for this kind of analysis. Each answer is set up as a comparison between two people, using simple adjectives to describe each person. You simply have to find the answer choice where the descriptions of the people are supported by synonyms in the passage. Choice G is incorrect because, though we can certainly infer that the woman is bitter and resentful from words such as: annoyed and

miserable, it is obvious that the narrator is not detached and uninterested from her multiple attempts to respond optimistically to her friend's qualms. Remember, the ACT likes to trap people into the thought process that if one part of an answer is correct, the rest of the answer must be correct. In this case, the first comparison was correct, but the second one was not. Choice H is incorrect because it cannot be reasonably inferred from the passage that the narrator is relaxed. She is obviously worried about her friend's emotional disposition and is trying to console her. Choice J is the most obviously wrong answer, as there is no support for the description of the narrator as angry, although she may be slightly discontented that her friend cannot dream. Choice F is the most correct answer because it is clear that the woman is quite frustrated by her ability not to dream through descriptions such as "sadly" and that the narrator is supportive through her attempts to console her friend in the 6th paragraph. This also implies that she is optimistic.

3) To answer this question, we need to refer to specific parts in the passage. Just look for the quality that is most supported as something that the woman desires. There is no direct evidence in the passage that the woman wishes to have dreams for relaxation, so Choice A can be eliminated. Choice C is incorrect because it is also not supported in the passage that the woman wants entertainment from her dreams. Rather, it seems that she is searching for something deeper and more meaningful than mere enjoyment and pleasure from her dreams. Choice D makes no sense in the context of the passage, and there is no support that the woman is seeking self control. Choice B makes the most sense. The woman wishes for dreams because she is seeking some higher level of understanding about herself (self-awareness), and the world around her. This sentiment is clearly seen to in the second sentence of the first paragraph.

4) This is a question that can best be answered by first seeking out all of the wrong answer choices. The question is asking which of the following sets of ideas does the door serve as a metaphor for. Choice F is wrong because there is no mention of the feelings of alertness and fatigue. The woman does not have problems sleeping; rather, she cannot dream. Choice G is wrong because it is clear through the overall theme of the passage that the woman wishes to have a dream in the first place, and the focus is not on whether the dream is a nightmare or not. Take care with answer choices such as

B.   In the first paragraph, the words "nightmare" and "door" are in close proximity.   To the unwary reader, this may seem like the description of the metaphor that the question is looking for.   Choice H is incorrect because it is obvious that the woman's problem is not passing the threshold between sleep and wakefulness.   Choice J is the only answer that makes sense in the context of the passage.   When the woman sleeps, her inability to dream can be represented by a obstructive door that leads to the dream world that she does not wish, or is unable, to go through.

5)   This citation question asks you to make a direct inference about information specifically given in the passage.   Look at the citation, and try to get a sense of the tone that the author is conveying.   Through the description of the long smooth wall where blows to its surface don't resound whatsoever, we can see that this is a description of futility.   Now you should try to find the answer choice that concisely echoes this sentiment.   Choice A is incorrect because this citation has nothing to do with altering a dream in progress, let alone describe a feeling.   Furthermore, if you could alter a dream, why would you continue to stare at the long, brown, smooth wall that is bothering you so much?   Choice B is incorrect because the answer choice does not describe a feeling and it is not shown in the citation how the brown wall causes the nightmare.   Rather, the wall is in it self worse than a nightmare, as no dreams can be experienced.   Choice D is incorrect because the excerpt in lines 10-13 certainly does not suggest a possibility of escape, as the brown wall appears to be impassable and immotile.   Choice C is the correct answer because the lines serve to convey the sense of despair that the wall induces by suggesting that the wall is something different, and possibly worse, than a nightmare.

6)   For this question, we need to have a general idea where the amniotic dream is referred to in the passage.   This happens to be near the end, specifically in the 12th paragraph (starting with line 71).   Now all that remains is to pick the answer choice that most directly restates a specific idea from this paragraph.   After reading this section again quickly, it is very easy to eliminate the wrong answer choices.   Choice F is wrong because it is said no where in this section that this happens to be the narrator's favorite dream.   (Remember, don't get the narrator and the woman mixed up! If you do, it would seem as if this story is indeed the narrator's favorite.)   Choice H is similarly wrong because it is not stated that the narrator

has had this dream several times. Choice J is wrong because it simply is not specifically stated that the woman wants to dream the narrators dream. In fact, it is stated in the last sentence of the passage that the woman would like to fly in her dream, jumping from tree top to tree top. Remember, don't stretch your thoughts too far when answering these questions. The right answer is always clearly stated in the passage, or enough information is given so that a direct inference that corresponds to the right answer can be made. Choice G is correct because it is stated explicitly in the first sentence of paragraph 12 that the woman likes this dream the best, which would obviously mean she is fond of hearing it.

7) This is a question that can be answered with a general knowledge of the passage and with specific citations within the passage. Why would the woman wish to dream? It is clear that she wishes to have the experience of being in the dream world, but also that she wishes she was not different from others in this regard. Choice A is completely wrong because it contradicts the main idea of the passage by stating that the woman is afraid of dreaming. Choice B is wrong because it is not stated anywhere that the woman believes that the narrator will abandon her due to her present situation. Rather, the narrator is doing the opposite by consoling her friend and even describing these interactions with her! Choice C is wrong because the woman clearly is not able to dream, let alone have nightmares. Choice D is the only answer that makes sense with regards to the general ideas presented in the passage because it states that the woman is afraid of being different from others. Furthermore, this sentiment can be directly inferred from the ninth paragraph (lines 57-58), where it is stated that the woman feels envy over this perceived "power" that others besides her have.

8) This question requires some inference based on information directly stated in the passage. The reference to the woman trying to dream the narrator's dreams is in paragraph 9. The correct answer choice will be the one that most accurately describes the information given in this paragraph. Choice F does not fit with the tone of this paragraph. The woman is not at all confrontational towards the narrator and does not show any significant power over the narrator. Rather, she conceals her efforts from the narrator. Choice G is wrong because the woman is clearly not enthusiastic and playful about having to dream other people's dreams. She is ashamed that she must do this, and she tries to keep it a secret. Choice H is wrong

because the woman is not precise in being able to dream the narrator's dreams because she cannot even dream at all! Choice J is the only choice that makes sense because it is evident from the fact that the narrator believes that the woman tries to dream her dreams with the lights off and behind closed doors that the woman is extremely self conscious and secretive about having to do this.

9) For this question, simply plug in the each of the answer choices where the word "humor" was and see which one sounds most reasonable. Choice A can be eliminated because it is not supported that the failed efforts to dream bring about personality changes, which are much more permanent. Choice B makes absolutely no sense because whim means desire, and the phrase "bad desire" is awkward. Choice D is wrong because it is clear that humor does not convey its normal meaning in this context. There is nothing comedic about this situation. Choice C is the correct answer because mood is temporary and this description works better with the temporary feeling of envy.

10) This question asks for a correct description of information directly present in the passage. A good way to tackle this problem is to quickly scan the passage looking for the key word "Kafka". Once you find it (paragraph 9), you simply must find the answer choice that paraphrases this information. Choice F is wrong because it says the exact opposite of what is presented in this paragraph. Kafka can convey dreams without much distortion, rather than diminishing them. Choice G is wrong because it is specifically stated that Kafka did not try to rationalize dreams. Choice J is also wrong because it is stated that Kafka can successfully convey dreams, and that this skill is an art. Choice H is correct because it is stated that Kafka can describe the most essential parts of dreams with out adulterating or rationalizing their content, so they keep their abstract character.

11) This question requires you to make a generalization of information given by a large piece of the passage. It is in the fourth paragraph where the passage explores the potential role of climate change in the course of history. It is clear from a quick scan of the remainder of the passage after the fourth paragraph that the author believes that climate change was not the primary motivator of historical change, but that its effects should still not be neglected. Knowing this, we can eliminate choice B because it is not stated anywhere that the author believes it is right that the effects of climate

change are ignored by scientists. Rather, he believes that some attention should be paid to the climate change during the period. Choice C is incorrect because even though this may not a completely false statement, it is not supported at all in the passage. The author does not mention the effect of climate change on modern civilization in Europe. Choice D, which states the direct opposite of choice B, should be eliminated as well. The author states in the fourth paragraph that the shaping of European civilization should NOT be directly attributed to the "little ice age". Choice A is the only answer that makes sense based on the author's statements in the passage. In paragraph 4, the author cautions against using the little ice age as a universal explanation for the dynamics of Europe during 1300-1850, whereas in paragraph 5, he notes that the correlation of climate change and the dynamics of human civilization should not be ignored completely.

12)   This question is easy because it just asks you to summarize the essence of the first paragraph in one concise statement. Choice A is wrong because it is stated that the period was characterized by wildly inconsistent weather. Choice B is incorrect because it is stated in the opening phrase before the passage even begins that the essay is about the climate during 1300-1850, which obviously was long after mammoths went extinct(though, as this answer choice hopes to do, it misleads you into thinking of the ice age that occurred while mammoths were still alive). Choice J is incorrect. Although interaction between oceans and the atmosphere is mentioned, it is not the key point of the paragraph. Choice H correctly describes the first paragraph as a whole. The main purpose of this paragraph is to state that climate conditions where quite ephemeral during this period, which is consistent with "frequent and short term climate shifts".

13)   This is an example of a direct citation question.   For these questions, it is usually necessary to read the lines directly before and after the citation to get a idea of the context of the citation.   After doing this, it is evident that the descriptions of weather of the type referred to in the passage are somewhat insightful, but not very useful for scientific analysis of weather patterns.   Choice A is wrong because it is implied that descriptions like this have some value. Choice B is wrong because though 18th century people may have been impressed by the weather, the primary effect of this statement is to show the inadequacy of such descriptions.   Choice C is wrong because it is not stated that these records were used back in the time

period to compare different storms. Choice D is correct because it states that notes taken in the past about weather are of little scientific use in the modern day, which is consistent with the context of the citation.

14) This is a simple chronology question, one of the easiest question types to answer in the reading section. The reason why this author mentions these events is because they are events of significance that overlap with the little ice age. Therefore, the only answer that makes sense is choice F, and all others can be eliminated.

15) This is a question that requires analyzing the citation and connecting it with general themes in the passage. The general idea presented in the passage is that this "ice age" can potentially cause long lasting consequences indirectly if not directly. With this in mind, the question is basically asking you to restate the idea presented in the lines. Choice B is wrong because no mention is made of the distinction between hunger and plentiful supplies of food   Choice C is wrong because it is not stated that food shortages were rare at the continental level, though the phrase "continent level scale" is mentioned. In fact, it can be inferred that frequent fluctuations in crop cycles meant that hunger was quite common. Choice D is incorrect because although this may have been a motivating factor, it is not a point that can be reasonably inferred solely from the passage. Choice A is correct because it is directly supported by the phrase "with consequences that could take decades to unfold" in the fourth paragraph. Be wary of deceiving answer choices that contain words that are in the passage. Quickly skimming though the passage, you may pick an answer choice because it has a few words from the passage, as is the case in choice C. Scan for words initially, but make sure you look closely at the material to eliminate wrong answers, for there is only one answer that is supported by the passage.

16) This question asks about information specifically in the passage based on a citation. Again, you should read past these lines to get an idea of the context of the citation. It will then be evident that the other answer choices don't describe the correct reason why the author mentions those events. Choice F is wrong because it is not stated that the entire western civilization could be threatened. In fact, it is stated in the passage that the entire civilization could not be

destroyed just because of this ice age, so this answer choice is a direct contradiction to information presented. Choice G is wrong because the citation not intended to be a criticism of the agriculture. Weather related damage is not due to the inadequacy of the agricultural methods, and is certainly not a point supported by the passage. Choice H is wrong because although environmental determinism is mentioned in the passage, it is not mentioned in the context of these lines. Choice J is the correct answer because it is directly stated right after the citation that climate shifts may have had a role in shaping modern Europe.

17) For this problem, we must look at the paragraphs where the debate about the role of climate change in the course of European history is started. This is the fourth paragraph and the 5th paragraph. Again, this is a question where we must find the one incorrect statement in the answer choices. At the bottom of the fifth paragraph, we see all the information that we need to answer the question. Choice A is wrong because it is stated directly that human ineptitude was a cause of the food crises. The same is true for choices B and C. Choice D is the correct answer because though the phrase "intellectually bankrupt" is mentioned, it is not used do describe potential causes of food shortages. Rather it is describing a theory that is no longer being studied. This is a clear trick that is aimed at students who would only take a quick glance at the words in the passage without looking at their context.

18) Where is the little ice age first mentioned in the passage? Since the little ice age is the main focus of the passage, it is a fair assessment that the little ice age is first mentioned in the first paragraph. It is stated here that the ice age was caused by "complex and not well understood interactions between the ocean and the atmosphere" With this information, we can now eliminate answer choices. Choice F is wrong because describing the mechanics of the little ice age as straightforward is a direct contradiction to information given in the paragraph. Choice H is wrong because it is not mentioned that the little ice age is not well studied today. The fact that there is a whole article about this ice age is evidence of at least some in depth study. Choice J is wrong because it is certainly not true that this little ice age was in any way beneficial to humans. Though it may or may not have been history changing, it certainly was a hardship that people in Europe had to contend with. Choice G is correct because it is directly stated in the first paragraph that complex

interactions between the ocean and atmosphere that are not well understood caused this little ice age. .

19)   We can find information of the elements of the little ice age by again looking at the first paragraph.   We are also again looking for the answer choice that has incorrect information.   Choice A is wrong because it is directly stated in this paragraph that the little ice age was characterized by heavy spring and early summer rains.   Choice B is wrong because it is stated that winters were intense and that there were easterly winds.   Choice C is wrong because droughts and light northeasterly winds are mentioned as descriptions of the little ice age. Choice D is correct because it is completely contradictory to the passage that the little ice age would be characterized by mild winters and a calm ocean, and is therefore not supported by the passage. Furthermore, if the world is in an ice age, it is obvious that there will be harsh winters.

20)   This question also references material within the first paragraph. At the end of the paragraph, there is a mention that the prolonged warming that characterizes today's weather is an anomaly.   This is exactly what is stated in choice G, so we can immediately eliminate all of the other answer choices.   For questions that don't ask for the answer choice that has an incorrect statement, the correct answer choice is information that is almost identical to what is found in the passage, with only a few words difference in some cases.

21)   What is a theme that is echoed most often throughout the passage regarding Louis Armstrong.   For much of the passage, the techniques that Louis Armstrong pioneered are mentioned, and his influence on many musical genres is noted.   The general tone of this message is obviously positive, so we can eliminate choice A because the passage does not state that Armstrong's emotional range was narrow.   Choice B is wrong because although the passage contends that Louis Armstrong had unparallel skills on the trumpet,. It did not mention that Armstrong was only characterized by soft and luminous tones.   Rather, he was recognized for the wide range of sounds he could create. Choice D is wrong because information provided in the passage shows that Armstrong's wonderful compositions were continually created beyond the 1920s.   Be wary of answer choices like these, as the phrase "mid to late 20s" is present in the 5th

paragraph in another context. Choice C is correct because it is clear from even a very general knowledge of the passage that Louis Armstrong pioneered many musical techniques that have influenced modern music. This is specifically referred to in the 5th paragraph when the passage mentions that Armstrong had influenced American music in general by the time of his death.

22) For this type of question, you must look for the information given by the answer choices within the passage. If it is present, then it is obviously a wrong answer. Choice F is wrong because multiple paragraphs are spent describing the groundbreaking techniques that Armstrong pioneered in jazz music. Choice G is wrong because it is stated in the first paragraph that his intricate improvisations made the jazz soloist stand out from the band. Choice H is wrong because it is stated in the third paragraph that Armstrong popularized "scat" singing. Choice J is the correct answer because no where in the passage are specific masterpieces of Armstrong's mentioned. The passage mainly focuses on his groundbreaking musical techniques.

23) In the context of the passage, the contribution that is mentioned or referred to most frequently can be assumed to be Armstrong's most important contribution to Jazz, at least in the author's opinion. What the author mentions most in the passage is Armstrong's knack for effortlessly and melodically soloing in jazz. Therefore, we can start eliminating choices. Choice A is wrong because though it is stated that Armstrong had played with the London Philharmonic, it is not implied that he conquered all of Europe musically, and it is stated that he mainly had an influence on American music. Choice C is wrong because King Oliver was only one of the many people with which Louis Armstrong played along. Choice D is wrong because it is not stated anywhere that Armstrong invented the blues sound. Rather, it is implied that he fused the blues genre with the jazz genre. Choice B is correct because it is clear that Armstrong's greatest contribution, according to the passage, was his pioneering improvisational technique, and much time is spent describing the virtuosic method with which Armstrong approached jazz trumpet.

24) It is important when answering this question not to pick the answer choice that mentions one piece of information that is within the paragraph. You must find the answer choice that best describes how this paragraph functions with regards to the rest of the passage. The

focus of the paragraph is on Armstrong's movement up the ranks of the music scene. Choice F is wrong because although it is stated that King Oliver was one of Armstrong's mentors, Oliver only represents one of the steps on the path that Armstrong took to become a renown jazz musician. Choice H is wrong because the opinions of Henderson and Oliver are not mentioned in this paragraph. Choice J is wrong because the paragraph doesn't serve solely to describe the growth of Armstrong's distinctive style while playing with Henderson. Choice G is correct because the events described in paragraph two are a description of Armstrong's rising career step by step.

25) All the details necessary to answer this question are contained within paragraph 4, and it is asking which detail is not mentioned in this paragraph. Choice A, B, and D are all directly stated in this paragraph. Choice C is not, however. Though Armstrong had much endurance in his playing, it is not stated that he played an all night show. Therefore, Choice C is the correct answer.

26) You should approach this question in the same way that you approached question 25. From the last paragraph, we get the impression that Armstrong's music reached many different environments, had an eclectic set of influences, and was enhanced by Armstrong's desire to have his audience get as much pleasure from music as he did. Choices G, H, and J all serve to summarize these ideas. However, it is not stated that Armstrong's goal was to reshape American music. It is implied that that was just a side effect of his intense enjoyment and passion for jazz music. Therefore, choice F is the correct answer.

27) This question ties into the last one. How did Armstrong want to make his audience feel when he played. According to the paragraph, Armstrong wanted to make his audience feel the pleasure that he felt by playing music. Choice A and B, awe and determination, do not describe Armstrong's goal; they are merely side effects of his enthusiastic performances. Choice D does not make any sense at all because Louis Armstrong's music was groundbreaking and was not intended to bring back nostalgic feelings. This is a point reaffirmed through out the passage. Choice C is correct because it is directly mentioned that Armstrong wanted his audience to feel the pleasure while listening to his music.

28) This question asks about a chronology of events described in the passage. This particular chronology, dealing with the location of Armstrong, can be found in paragraph 3. It is stated at the end of the paragraph that Armstrong finally settled in New York in 1929, and was based there for the rest of his career. New Orleans was where he originally came from, and Chicago was one of the places he stayed while moving early in his career. It is not mentioned in the passage that Armstrong lived in Paris. Therefore, choice G is the correct answer.

29) This question asks what the purpose of the detail presented with in the citation is with regards to the passage. As always with specific citation questions, it is essential to read around the citations as well. In this paragraph, we get the idea that Louis Armstrong was an extremely versatile and staminate trumpeter . The mention of the glissando is used to describe the technical skill of Armstrong on this instrument, and how he had this skill to such a degree that people thought it was not possible to play on a regular trumpet. Choice B is wrong because it is clear that Armstrong has a clear mastery of his instrument to pull these techniques off. Choice C is wrong because it is implied that Armstrong was doing all of these techniques on an unmodified trumpet. Choice D is wrong because it is stated no where that Armstrong created the glissando. Though he had mastered the technique, it was not his invention. Choice A is the correct answer because this citation is meant to illustrate how adept Armstrong was at his instrument, which is the idea conveyed in this choice.

30) This is a tone question. According to the description provided in the lines, how could the actions of an orchestra in response to Louis Armstrong influences be described?   It is stated that the orchestra, along with other artists, subconsciously swing in rhythm. They certainly don't do this reluctantly, and they apparently don't do it consciously. Optimistically does not work as a descriptor in this context. Choice H, or unconsciously, is the correct answer.

31) This is another type of question where you must find the choice that is not supported by the passage. The idea of qi is mentioned in the first three paragraphs. In the first paragraph, it is mentioned that the flow of qi throughout the body is essential to good health. Therefore, you can eliminate choice D, because a disruption in the

flow of qi would cause malfunction and illness, according to the passage. In paragraph three, the effects of the lack, or excess of qi, are described. Choice A can be eliminated because it is stated that "Yin", or the shortage of qi, is linked to certain medical maladies. Similarly, choice B can also be eliminated because it shows how "Yang", or an excess of qi, can lead to other bad symptoms. Choice C is the correct answer because it is not stated anywhere in the description of qi what would happen if the temperature of qi changes. It is, however, stated that qi is a warm substance, and different levels of it cause different symptoms characteristic of different temperatures.

32) This question asks for you to concisely state the information presented in lines 35-45. Simply pick the statement that best accomplishes this. We can do this easily by identifying the "gist" of lines 35-45, which is that acupuncture at certain points in the body sends impulses to the limbic system and pituitary glands and results in the secretion of pain relieving chemicals. Choice G is wrong because it is stated that the impulse from the stimulated nerve must travel up the spinal cord and reach the brain before pain is relieved. Choice H is wrong because it is stated that the chemicals are released only after the signal is passed up to the pituitary gland. No chemicals amplify signals sent to the spinal cord. Choice J is incorrect because it is a direct contradiction to the presented information. The nerve stimulation does not inhibit signals being sent to the brain, nor does it numb the spine. Rather, it does the opposite by triggering a signal transduction to the brain through the spinal cord. Choice F is the correct answer because it most nearly states the "gist" of lines 35-45: signals are sent up to the brain through the spinal cord and trigger chemical release.

33) To answer this question, we must not for what kind of ailments has this study of acupuncture been confirmed with. For this, you should use the technique of reading around the stated citation to get more information. It is evident after doing this that the study describes how acupuncture triggers the release of endorphins, which help block pain. Therefore, choice A and choice B are wrong because nausea and blurred vision are not descriptions of pain, but rather, other forms of discomfort. Also, it is stated that nausea and blurred vision are not affected by the endorphin system in the subsequent paragraphs. Choice D can be eliminated because the immune system is not mentioned in the passage whatsoever. Choice

C is correct because the study on the triggering of endorphins would be related to headaches, which are obviously a type of pain.

34)   For this question, we must find the place where the volunteer experiment is described.   The goal of this experiment was to see if a specific acupuncture point could produce the same concentration of brain activity in a particular area of the brain as shining light into the subjects' eyes.   Corresponding foot acupuncture points were tested, as well as random points on the foot, such as the big toe.   Now that we have this understanding, we can eliminate answer choices. Choice F is wrong because brain activation maps were the result of the experiment, not the thing that the volunteers were exposed to, and this had no effect on brain activity.   Choice G is wrong because subjects were exposed to light, and the color was evident on the brain activation maps, so color had nothing to do with brain activity. Choice H is wrong because it was shown that big toe stimulation, which was used as a control, was not a trigger for brain activity. Choice J is correct because it was shown in the experiment that stimulation of acupuncture points on certain places on the outside of the foot caused increased brain activity in the desired region.

35)   What is the main idea conveyed in the last paragraph of the passage?   As a description of the usefulness of the experiments described in the previous paragraph, it basically states that some questions about acupuncture were answered, while more questions about acupuncture as a whole were raised. Choice A is wrong because it is specifically stated that more questions have been raised about the mechanisms by which acupuncture works.   Choice C is wrong because the experimenter did not question the validity of older studies; he merely set out to conduct further research on acupuncture. Choice D is wrong because it was shown that some acupuncture point are definitely correlated with increased brain activity in certain regions, a major discovery.   Choice B is the correct answer because it correctly restates the idea of the paragraph: some questions were answered, and others were posed.

36)   This question requires you to refer back to the description of yin and yang in the third paragraph. After looking quickly through this, it is clear that yin and yang are directly related to the quantities of qi in ones system.   F, G, and H are therefore incorrect.   Though those

effects may be correlated with yin and yang, yin and yang are solely dependent on qi, so choice J is the correct answer.

37) This is another question where you need to look at the information on yin and yang in the third paragraph! From the description of yin and yang, it is implied that excess yin produces melancholic symptoms, while excess yang produces hyperactive symptoms. Agitation, fast pulse, and fever are all symptoms of someone with a yang condition. A pale face, however, is not caused by too much yang. Therefore, choice A is the correct answer.

38) For this question type, we can use the technique of substituting the word in the passage with the words in the answer choices. Choice F is wrong because extracted does not make sense in the context of the sentence, as nothing is being extracted in this situation. Choice G is not the right answer because concentrated in this context is used to describe quantity rather than a state of mind. Choice J is incorrect because "concentrated" isn't referring to a topic or information, but the nerves at acupuncture points. Choice H is the correct answer because gathered together would fit properly in this context: ....where nerves are highly gathered together". Much of the time, picking the choice that sounds least awkward is the best strategy for these types of questions.

39) For this question, we need to look at the paragraph that describes Cho's experiment. At the end of the paragraph, it is mentioned that the stimulation of the big toe is used as a control to make sure stimulation of non acupoints does not cause the same brain activity. Choice A is wrong because the brain activity that was caused by the light was compared to that caused by acupoint stimulation. Choice B is wrong because the vision acupoint stimulation was the actual process that was being verified, not the placebo. Choice C is wrong because there is no mention of an eye examination chart in the experiment. Choice D is the correct answer because it is stated that stimulating a non acupoint on the foot and seeing the subsequent brain activity was used as a placebo control in the experiment.

40) This question can be answered by looking at the first sentence in the last paragraph. It is stated clearly that, similarly to other initial

experimental studies, Cho's experiment raised more questions than it answered.   Choice F is wrong because it is clear that the answers that are raised often require new experimentation.   Choice H may be true but is not mentioned within the paragraph.   Choice J is wrong because it is not stated that most experiments end with the realization that the wrong questions are being asked.   Choice G is the correct answer because this is exactly what is stated in the last paragraph regarding Cho's experiment.

ACT SCIENCE REASONING STRATEGY
by **Rajiv Raju**

Key Science Strategies

-No background knowledge is expected. Every thing needed to answer the questions will be in the passage.

-The passages may look very complex, but the questions are usually very simple.

-Any important terminology will be italicized and easy to find. The definition usually follows the italicized word.

- Your objective is not to thoroughly understand the passage, but to answer the questions correctly. Unfortunately, the time limits in the science section make it almost impossible to fully understand all the passages. However, it is possible to answer many of the questions without fully understanding the passage by just looking at the data. Trying to fully understand the passage may remove your focus from answering the questions which is all that matters for the score.

The science reasoning test presents scientific descriptions/data and tests your ability to analyze this information. Having science classes will help you develop the skill that this section tests, but you do not need to memorize any facts or formulas. All the information that you will need is presented to you in the test.

Of the 40 questions in the science reasoning test from the booklet, we found two questions that required the student to make common sense or very basic prior knowledge assumptions. In question 11, we must assume that the purpose of using the plastic water bottle is that it is clear as opposed to the aluminum can.   In question 18, we need to know that photosynthesis occurs in chloroplast. The information and assumptions needed to answer all the other 38 questions are explicitly stated in the test.

As with the Reading section, many students will not be able to finish this section. If you are having difficulty finishing this section, you may want to try and answer some questions without reading the entire passage. To prove that this works at least on some questions try the following test: Try to answer questions 6 to 10 by only looking at the graphs. Do not read any of the paragraphs. For question 6 look at Figure 2 and you should be able to answer the question by looking at the depth chart and the different reference points of the different sites. Now try question 7. Graphical analysis can be used to find the answer to this question, even if we do not know the exact definition of the strange looking symbol. Similarly questions 8, 9, and 10 can all be answered based on the graphs alone. We do not need to look at the extensive introductory paragraph or even refer to figure 1! In this case, every question in the passage could be answered by just looking at quantitative information in the figures. This technique will not always work, but it might be worth trying if you are running out of time. For passages such as the conflicting-hypothesis scenario, some skimming is required to answer the questions. The skimming in this section should be restricted to finding the most general idea of what the scientist or student is trying to convey. As with the other sections of the test, always answer every question even if you are running short of time and cannot even look at the question. This is critical for the science reasoning section, where the score drops drastically for each wrong answer, Remember, there is no penalty for guessing on ANY of the ACT sections, so give yourself a 25% chance at getting those last questions right by filling in some answer!

The recommended strategy for the science reasoning test is as follows:

If the passage has a lot of text and few tables and graphs, just read the whole passage as quickly you can and then answer the questions as you would with the reading section. When you answer the questions you must go back to the passage to find evidence to support your answer. If you find evidence to contradict a choice, eliminate it from consideration. There will always be evidence in the passage to support the correct answer. **Do not talk yourself into an answer that can not be explicitly supported in the passage.**

If you see a lot of graphs and tables of data, go straight to the questions and try to answer as many of the questions as possible based on the data alone, reading the text only as needed. If you do look at the charts before reading the questions, only do so to look at the variables or the axes for this data. Any **important terminology will be italicized and easy to find. The definition usually follows the italicized word.** Once again, you must only pick the answers that can be supported by the data. In the sections with many graphs and tables, understanding every aspect of the concepts outlined is almost always not necessary. **Your main objective is to answer the questions correctly, not to understand all of the jargon and concepts in the passage. Do not let the jargon scare you. The questions are usually easy.** Sufficient information about the concepts can be deduced directly from the charts. What is most important in these chart-based passages is to understand the variables of the experiment and the effect of the variables on each other.

The next chapter goes through all 40 questions in the Science section of the booklet and illustrates how, in each case, information from the passage supports the one correct answer and often contradicts the incorrect answers. Remember, the ACT places trick answer choices in the test that the test makers know can be incorrectly inferred by the test takers. They know how our brains tick, in other words, at least with regards to test taking. So don't fall for the incorrect answer patterns. The answer is ALWAYS explicitly stated in the passage, or can be reasonably inferred from the data given.

ACT SCIENCE EXPLANATIONS
By **Rajiv Raju**

Please refer to the questions in the Science component of the practice test (Form 0964E) in official ACT booklet, Preparing for the ACT .

1)   Like very many science reasoning questions, we can answer this problem without even reading the background information and solely looking at the figure.   First it helps to just glance at figure 1 for a moment and see how its information categorized.   It appears that the picture shows graduated degree values over a depiction of earth with its multiple layers. Luckily for us, the information we need to answer this question is clearly stated on this graph, and we don't need to interpret the direction of the wave lines. All you have to do is find the region where 125 degrees is.   It says clearly there that neither p waves or s waves are received at this point. Choice A and B are wrong because P waves and S waves are not received by the seismograph individually.   Choice C is wrong because both waves are not received together by the seismograph at this point.   Choice D is correct because it correctly states that neither P waves or S waves make it to the seismograph at this point.

2)   For this problem, we need to note two important features of figure 1.   First, you should notice that p wave paths are indicated by the solid arrows.   Also you need to identify where the boundary between the mantle and the core is.   This boundary is represented by the outside of the darkened circle within the larger circle representing earth.   Now that we have an idea of how the information we need is organized, we can eliminate answer choices.   Choice F is wrong because it is clear that solid arrows are penetrating through the core, as opposed to being stopped in their tracks.   Choice H is wrong because the P-waves are still P-waves when they emerge out through the other side of the core and are recorded by the seismograph.   Choice J is wrong because there are only two types of waves mentioned in this diagram, and there is no evidence that these waves are transformed into some wave form other than the P and S waves. Choice G is the correct answer because we can see that as the P-waves enter the core, they start to lose their straight character on

the diagram, indicating that they are being refracted within the core.

3) For this problem, we need to use some linear extrapolation and a little common sense in eliminating answer choices. Look at figure three and notice that the S wave graph is much different than the P wave graph in that it takes much more time for s waves to reach a particular point away from the focus than P waves. However, the graph only goes up to 10,000 km away from the earthquake surface. Because the question is asking us to find what the difference in wave arrival times is at a distance larger than is graphed we can use the time difference corresponding to the 10,000 km value on the x axis as a starting point. To reach the seismograph 10,000 km away from the earthquake, it takes the P wave 12 minutes. For the S wave, we can do some extrapolation and estimate that the wave would take about 24 minutes to reach the seismograph 10,000 km from the earthquake focus. This obviously is a difference of 12 minutes. From the trend in the data, it is clear that as distance from the earth quake focus increases, the difference between the arrival times of the two types of waves increases. Therefore, we would expect the difference between the arrival times of the P and S waves to be greater at 10,500 km away from the focus. By this type of reasoning, we can eliminate all the answer choices except the one that states that the difference in arrival times between the waves is greater than 10 minutes, or Choice D, which is the only accurate description of the data.

4) This question again requires a small amount of common sense and graph reading ability. It is fairly obvious that the time the earth quake starts at focus would correspond to the start of the graphing of the waves movement, which is at 0 km from the earth quake, and 0 mins of wave travel, or the point (0,0) on the x-y axis. Choice G, H, and J don't make sense because these answer choices describe waves that have already started moving away from the focus. Therefore, choice F is the correct answer because it correctly describes the starting point of the earthquake, at 0 km from the focus 0 mins of wave travel away from the focus.

5) This is one of the few science reasoning questions that require a minimal knowledge background. In this case, you must know what the term amplitude means. In case you don't know, amplitude is the height of a wave from its resting position to hits highest value within a given period. The relative amplitude would

therefore be a description of the average amplitude of a graph that has varying amplitude levels at different times. With this information we can answer the question. Choice B is wrong because the amplitude of the P-waves is not larger than those of the S waves, as the graph of the S waves reaches higher than that of the P waves. Choice C is wrong because the P waves are not the same amplitude as the S waves that arrive later. Choice D is incorrect because it is obvious by the shape of the P and S waves that they do not have an amplitude of zero, which would be indicated by a straight line on figure two. Choice A is the correct answer because the P waves are smaller in amplitude than the S waves that come after them.

6) Though it is a good idea to very briefly glance at the introductory paragraph in every passage, we do not need any information in this paragraph to answer this particular question. What we do need to do, however, is quickly note some key features on figure 2. First, notice that lake clay is indicated by the light clay color. Also, because the y-axis of the graph in figure 2 represents length, we can use this as an indicator of the thickness or thinness of an area. Obviously, the point where the lake clay occupies the least amount of elevation is where the thinnest area of lake clay will be. Site 1 has the second largest amount of lake clay deposit out of the other sites described in the answer choices, so Choice G can be eliminated. Site 2 has a lesser amount of deposit than site 1, but still does not have the smallest amount of deposit, so choice H can be eliminated. Choice J, or Grand Forks, can also be eliminated because it is only the second thinnest deposit. Choice F, or Winnipeg, is the correct answer because this is the area where there is the least amount of lake clay deposit.

7) For this question, we simply need to understand and correctly interpret the graphs. The complicated looking equation at the bottom of figure 3 is not necessary at all for this problem. We do, however, need to note that the y axis describing depth is going from high values to low values when reading from a normal orientation. Also, the values for the oxygen are getting less negative along the x axis, which means that they are getting larger. We are looking for the depth where there is the smallest oxygen level. From the data on the graphs, it appears that as depth decreases, the oxygen content of the water increases in lake clay. Therefore, we would expect the oxygen content to be lowest at deeper depths for lake clay. Where is the point where

the lowest amount of oxygen that can be measured is located? At all of the sites, this point is between 20 and 30 meters. Lake clay does not have any measurable oxygen at 30-40 meters of depth, so choice D can be eliminated. Also higher depths will have more oxygen content for lake clay, so choices A and B are wrong. Choice C, or 20-30 meters, correctly describes where the lowest amount of measurable oxygen concentration is located.

8) Think of figure two in terms of a graph again. Look at the relationship between the lake clay and glacial till moving backwards from Grand Forks to Site 3. As the thickness of the lake clay increases, the thickness of the glacial till clearly decreases. Choice F is wrong because as the lake clay thickness increases, the glacial till is always decreasing and is never increasing. Thus we can also eliminate Choice H. It is also evident that the glacial till thickness does not remain the same as the lake clay thickness increases, so choice G can be discarded. Choice J is the correct answer because it correctly describes what is occurring to the glacial till as the lake clay increases in thickness: its thickness decreases and only decreases during this period.

9) For this question, we should look at the figure two to see the dynamics of the glacial till from site 1 to 3. We can see that the elevation increases from site 1 to site 2, and drops off again to a point lower than the glacial till at site one at site 3. Now we need to find the graph that best illustrates this trend. Choice A is wrong because the bars indicate that site one has the highest elevated glacial till, and sites 2 and 3 see a subsequent and continuous drop in elevation of glacial till. Choice B is incorrect because it indicates that site 1 has the glacial till with the lowest elevation. Choice D is wrong because the graph in this choice indicates that site one has the glacial till with the highest elevation, while according to figure 2, site 2 has the highest glacial till elevation. Choice C is the correct answer because it correctly shows the relationship shown in figure two: a slight increase in elevation from site 1 to site 2, and a large drop in elevation to a level lower than site 1 in site 3.

10) This question requires a bit of linear interpolation because we are not given an oxygen concentration value for a depth of 3 meters in the figure 3 graphs. According to the data, what two points are around the area where the content point of oxygen at 3 meters would most likely be. These points are clearly located at

the values slightly beyond -18 and before -14, respectively. We can now eliminate all the answer choices that are not between -18 and -14, which are choices F, G, and H. Choice J, or -15 is a reasonable answer because the dot corresponding to a -15 oxygen content is around a value of 3 meters for depth. The last point on the graph very closely resembles this description.

11)   For this question, you need to think about why a clear plastic bottle would have been useful in this experiment. If you read through the short paragraph describing experiment 3, you should notice that they mention "bubbles being visible" on many occasions. This is a cue that visibility of bubbles is important for this experiment, and that this experiment was probably conducted to see the state of the liquid bubbles during different steps of the procedures outlined in the previous experiments. Choice A is wrong because there was no quantitative measurement of how fast the bottle rolled down the incline, so there was no accurate way to measure how much faster plastic rolled as opposed to aluminum. Choice C is wrong because 1 Liter of liquid was added to the bottle, which was the same amount of liquid present in the aluminum can. Choice D is wrong because it is not mentioned at all that the bottle had thicker walls, and it is not clear that the integrity of the bottle was important for these experiments. Choice B is correct because it can be most reasonably inferred that the purpose of experiment 3 was to see how the different experimental procedures such as shaking and rolling effected the amount of bubbles in the bottle.

12)   This is a very simple question that asks you to find similar numbers on tables 1 and 2. Obviously, you should only look at the "before shaking" section of these tables. After looking at the 5 trials, you can see that trials 1, 3, and 5 had the same roll time. Choices F, G, and H are wrong because 2 did not have a common roll time with trials 1,3,4, or 5. Choice J is the correct answer because those two trials had the same roll time. This is an unusually simple science reasoning problem, but always be wary for tricks in all problems.

13)   For this question, when referring to table 1, we must understand the variable that is being tested, or the control variable. The only control variable is the roll time, so that is the only thing piece of data that can be analyzed from this experiment. Choice A can be eliminated because it makes an describes a result with regards to the number of bubbles present. Since this

was not measured in this experiment, this result can not be verified. Similarly, choice B is wrong because it refers to the mass of the can, which was also not measured in the experiment. Now we must see whether shaking the can affected roll time, which is the only variable that was measured in this experiment. It is clear that shaking the can increased roll time, so choice C is wrong, and Choice D is the correct answer.

14) For this question, though experiment 2 is mentioned, we must refer to another experiment for the information necessary to pick an answer. Recall from experiment 1 what the purpose of the study was. Only roll time was measured in this experiment, and the number of bubbles was inconsequential. Therefore, the results from experiment 1 cannot help us answer this question. Choices F and G can be eliminated because they both refer to experiment 1. We need to find an experiment that gives us results that show how many bubbles are left over after two hours of stagnation, as this was the condition that the bottle in trial 5 was subject to. Since the only other experiment to look at is experiment 3, we should look at it and see that there were most likely no bubbles left over after the bottle was left to sit for 2 hours and was tested before shaking. Choice J makes no sense because according to the results of experiment 3, the bubbles could not last beyond 2 hours, let alone 3 hours. Choice H is correct because it correctly states that the bubbles lasted for less than two hours, so there were probably no bubbles present immediately prior to the testing before shaking.

15) This question requires some careful analysis of the data presented in trials 4 and 5. Judging by the information we got from experiment 3, after 2 hours, no bubbles would be left in the can or bottle. If we look again at the procedure for experiment 2, we can see that trial four was conducted 15 minutes after the can was shaken. It is stated in experiment 3 that 15 minutes after shaking, there were still some bubbles present in the bottle. As the data trends show, more bubbles correlates with longer rolling time. Therefore, the rolling time of a bottle that stood for 2 hours should be less than the bottle in trial 4, which stood for only 15 minutes. This means that the time had to be less than 1.86 seconds. B, C and, D can therefore be eliminated because these times are greater than or equal to 1.86 seconds. Choice A correctly states that the roll time of a bottle that has sat for 2 hours after trial 5 must be less than 1.86 secs.

16) This question can be answered solely with information found in the results of experiment 3. From these results, we cam see that there were still bubbles after 15 minutes of stagnation, but by 2 hours, the bubbles were gone. We can deduce from this that sometime between 15 minutes and 2 hours, bubbles cease to form with in the bottle. Choice F and G are wrong because they are under 15 minutes, and choice J is wrong because it is referring to a time above 2 hrs. Choice H is correct because it is in the range where bubbles would be reduced to a number small enough so that they didn't effect roll time.

17) For this question, we need to use information from one figure to interpret data in another table. We should not that the solid line in figure 1 represents chlorophyll b. Because this graph has absorbance as its y axis variable, the point on the x axis where the graph of chlorophyll b is highest will represent the correct wavelength. We can see that this wavelength is a little higher than 475 nanometers. With this information, we can now look at table 1 to see what color 475 nm corresponds to. Choice B is wrong because 500 nm-565 nm out of the range of 475 nm, so this color of light cannot correspond to the highest absorption by chlorophyll b. This means that Choices C and D are wrong because they are also out of the range of 475 nm. Choice A is correct because the range of 430 nm-500 nm is obviously where 475 nm would be, which corresponds to a blue color.

18) This is an example of a question that requires a very minimal amount of prior knowledge. An average high schooler should know that photosynthesis occurs in chloroplasts. If by some small chance you did not know this piece of common knowledge, you could deduce from words such as chlorophyll that choloroplasts are probably related to chlorophyll and the photosynthetic reactions. Therefore, Choices G, H, and J are incorrect because they have nothing in common with the reactions of photosynthesis, and Choice F is correct.

19) This question requires us to look at figure 2 and see which nm value corresponds to a photosynthesis rate that is higher than the rate at the given wavelength of 670 nm. We can do this by simply seeing where the graph goes above the 100% mark for rate. This occurs in the region between 420 nm and about 460 nm and again in the region between 670 and 680 nm. By making this quick assessment of the data, we now have ranges that we can use to eliminate answer choices. Choice A is incorrect

because 400nm is not within either range of acceptable values. Choice C and Choice D are incorrect for the same reasons. Therefore, choice B is correct because 430 nm is between 420 nm and 460 nm.

20) This is another question that requires a bit of prior knowledge to answer. This consists of knowing that the purpose of photosynthesis is to create a sugar molecule from solar energy. Look at the products of photosynthesis, and you will see the resultant products are sugar($C_6H_{12}O_2$), water(H_2O), and Oxygen gas(O_2). Choice F is wrong because fat is not one of the products of photo synthesis. Choice H is wrong because proteins contain some elements that are not even in the photosynthesis equation, such as nitrogen. Choice J is wrong because nucleic acids also contain nitrogen, which is not in the photosynthesis equation. Choice G is the correct answer because it correctly states that sugar is produced in photosynthesis.

21) This is another question where information obtained from one figure must be used to get more information from another figure. The figure where we would find which wavelength would yield the highest rate of photosynthesis is figure 2. This wave length is 440 nm. Using this value, we can go to figure 1 find the best description of the graph at this particular wavelength. Choice A is incorrect because the lowest relative absorption by chlorophyll a is a region from 500-550nm. Choice B is incorrect because the wavelength at which chlorophyll b has the least absorbance is 400 nm. Choice D is incorrect because the highest absorbance by chlorophyll b occurs at a wavelength slightly beyond 475 nm. Choice C is the correct answer because the highest absorbance by chlorophyll, or about 67, occurs at 440 nm, which is when photosynthetic rate is the highest.

22) To answer this question, we need to refer to the chart in experiment 1 and see what the resultant density is when only ethanol is present in the flask. The first liquid solution has the property that we need to answer the question: 100% ethanol in weight. The density is listed as 0.793 g/m. Choices F, H, and J can then be eliminated, and Choice G is the correct answer because it correctly states 0.793 g/mL.

23) This question requires a small amount of common sense and analysis of information from multiple charts. It requires that you can deduce that a material is less dense than the another material

if it floats in the other material. This is the basis of experiment 3, even though it is not explicitly stated. For PA-11, the first liquid that it floats in is liquid 6. If we look at table 2 in experiment 2, we can see that the density of liquid 6 is 1.05 g/mL. Using the assumption that a floating object has less density than the material it is floating in, we can infer that PA-11 has a density that is less than 1.05 g/mL. Since PA-11 sinks in liquid 5, which is the next densest liquid at .999 g/mL, we can further deduce that the density of PA-11 is between .999 g/mL and 1.05 g/mL. We can then eliminate answers A, B, and D, which all have density values that don't make sense. We are then left with choice C, which has the correct density range.

24) For this question, we need to see a relationship that is present within experiment 2. On table two, we can see that as the mass of the solution in the graduated cylinder increases, so does the density of the solution. Now we must do some extrapolation of this data. In general, the masses of the solution are increasing at about 3 grams per solution and the densities are increasing at about 0.05-0.06 g/mL for each solution. Choice F is wrong because a density of 1.25 g/mL would mean that the density of the liquid has gone down as the mass of the liquid has gone up, which is not supported by the trend in the data. Choice G is wrong because this increase is too small for an increase in mass of about 3 grams. Choice J is wrong because, judging by the data, an increase in mass by about 3 grams would not yield an increase in density by 0.11 g/mL. Choice H is the correct answer because it shows an increase of 0.06 g/mL in density, which is consistent with an increase of 3 grams for the mass of the solution.

25) To answer this question, you need to understand what "R" and "S" mean in experiment 3. R refers to a rising sample of plastic, and S refers to a sinking sample of plastic. From all of the data shown for liquids 1 through 4, which are all denser than the liquid before it, an S never shows up after an R. This makes sense because something should not rise in a certain liquid and sink in a denser liquid. The only choice where this is the case is choice B, and all the other choices are reasonable sets of results. Therefore, choice B is the correct answer.

26) This is another science question that requires a small amount of common sense. All we need to know is the definition of tare, which is in the description of the first experiment (setting the scale

to 0.000 grams). Now that we have this information, we can eliminate the answer choices that do not make sense. Choice G is wrong because setting the scale to zero would not aid directly in finding the density of the graduated cylinder, nor is it even necessary to find the density of the graduated cylinder. Only the density of the liquid within the graduated cylinder was needed. Choice H is wrong because a process that affects the starting mass on a scale would not help in determining when a correct volume has been achieved, as mass and volume are completely different units. Choice J is also wrong because taring the scale would not help determine when all of a substance has been dissolved. Only a visual or chemical test would determine if that has occurred. Choice F is the answer that makes the most sense because if the scale is tared after the cylinder is placed, then the mass of the substances can be directly measured, and the step of having to account for the mass of the cylinder would be eliminated.

27) For this question, we need to use our understanding of "R" and "S" that we needed to answer question 25. We also only need the information in Experiment 3. There are two parts to the answer: the actual answer, and the explanation for the answer. For the first round of elimination, we must determine whether polycarbonate is in fact denser than PA-6. With the knowledge that an object that rises in a liquid is less dense than the liquid, and the fact that liquids 1-10 are larger in density than the liquids proceeding them, we can definitively determine that polycarbonate is the denser material because it sinks in a liquid that PA-6 floats in. Choices A and C can immediately be eliminated because they state incorrectly that polycarbonate is not denser than PA-6. After looking at the remaining choices that start with "yes", we can see that Choice D is incorrect because its statement is illogical. If polycarbonate was the denser material, it would not rise in a liquid that the less dense material sunk in. Furthermore, this statement is not supported by the data in experiment 3 at all. Choice B is correct because it would make sense that because polycarbonate is a denser material than PA-6, it would potentially sink in a liquid that PA-6 floated in, which is the scenario that is supported by the experimental data.

28) For this question, we need to refer to the chart in experiment 1 with the + and - signs and understand that + means that fermentation occurred, and - means that fermentation did not occur for both types of fermentation. If even one + sign is present

under lactose, that qualifies as a type of fermentation.   This is the basis of the trick in choice F, which states that fermentation only occurs in species B.   If you are not careful, you may choose this answer because it is the only case where two + are present, which merely indicates that species B does both types of fermentation. Choice G is wrong because species C did not go through either type of fermentation, which is indicated by 2 - signs.   Choice J is wrong because it has already been established that species C did not go through any type of fermentation.   Choice H is the correct answer because according to the data, species B and D both have one or more + signs, indicating they went through some sort of fermentation in lactose.

29)   This is a rather tricky science question to tackle, as it requires careful inference of information from the data presented in Table 2.   Look at the pattern of + and - signs within the chart. All the useful information for this problem is present within the first 2 combinations.   If you look carefully, you will notice that though both the first combinations have species A, the fermentation patterns change with the addition of B and C.   In the case of the first combination, both types of fermentation occur in lactose broth, while in the second combination, both types of fermentation occur in the sucrose broth.   Therefore, it is safe to assume that species B was necessary for fermentation in lactose broth, and species C was necessary for fermentation in sucrose broth, so if both were mixed, the fermentations would occur in both sucrose and lactose.   Choice A is wrong because it shows that fermentation would not occur in sucrose broth.   Choice B is wrong because it shows that a combination of B and C would not ferment in lactose broth.   Choice D is wrong because it shows that no fermentation would occur whatsoever which is contrary to results that show that species B and C performed both types of fermentation in either sucrose or lactose.   Choice C is correct because it correctly states that both types of fermentation would occur in both mediums because B can ferment in lactose, while C can ferment in sucrose.

30) To answer this question, we simply need to find the results on the chart that correspond to this qualitative description of the data. Which species does both types of fermentation in lactose broth, but does neither in sucrose broth?   Species A doesn't ferment in either sucrose or lactose broth, so choice F can be eliminated. Species C does the opposite of the description: it does fermentation in sucrose, but not in lactose.   Therefore, choice H

can be eliminated. Species D does acidic fermentation in both broths, but does not do both types of fermentation in either broth, so choice J is incorrect. This leaves us with Choice G, which is the correct answer because species B does not ferment in sucrose, but does both types of fermentation in lactose.

31) For this question, we must simply pick the answer choice that makes sense with the data given. We do not have to give an explanation as to why the organisms act synergistically; that explanation is already given to us. So we are just to check the validity of each of the statements and see which answer choice has a completely valid description. Choice A is wrong because acid was clearly produced by both species in sucrose broth. Choice B is wrong because acid was produced by species D in lactose broth. Choice C is wrong because species C produced CO_2 in lactose. Choice D is the correct answer because CO_2 was not produced by each species individually in lactose broth, but when both species were mixed, CO_2 was produced in lactose broth.

32) This question is simply asking you to chose the correct visual description based on data given in experiment 1. However, we also need to know that a gas bubble within the Durham tube indicates that CO_2 fermentation occurred and that a yellow solution indicates that acidic fermentation occurred. On Table 1, it is shown that Species D was able to go through acidic fermentation but not CO_2 fermentation in sucrose. We can now eliminate incorrect pictures. Choice H is incorrect because though the picture indicates that the broth was yellow (acid produced), a gas bubble was produced, when the data states that CO_2 was not produced and acid was produced. Choice F is incorrect because though it correctly shows that no CO_2 was produced, it incorrectly shows that acid was not produced by indicating a red solution. Choice J is incorrect because CO_2 as well as acid were not produced according to this diagram. Choice G is the correct answer because the lack of a bubble in the picture indicates that CO_2 was not produced, while the yellowing of the solution indicates that acid was formed.

33) The definition of a synergistic relationship in the context of experiment 2 is that the two bacteria must be able to breakdown sugar by both forms of fermentation when they are mixed together. If a true synergistic relationship is present, this combination of bacteria must be able to break down all types of

sugar with both types of fermentation. Therefore, we can eliminate choice A because it states that there is a synergistic relationship between A and C because acid and CO2 were produced from only sucrose but not lactose. Choice B is wrong because the statement is incorrect; no fermentation occurred with the mixture of A and C within lactose. Choice C is wrong because CO2 was produced in sucrose by fermentation. Choice D is correct because it correctly states that the hypothesis can not validated because acid and CO2 was not formed in the lactose solution, which is classified as a sugar.

34) The conflicting scientists passages require a somewhat different approach. A quick skim to get the main ideas of the arguments from each passage is essential. What is the main idea of the DNA hypothesis? Genes are made of DNA. It is already established that genes have chromosomes. So if the amount of DNA increases, so will the number of genes, and the number of chromosomes as well. Choice F is wrong because it is stated that amino acids are integral parts of proteins, and it is not implied that protein amount increases from cell type to cell type along with the amount of DNA. Choice G is wrong because it also refers to amino acids increasing in amount along with DNA. Choice J is incorrect because the assumption of both of the hypothesis' are that there are no chromosomes in the cytoplasm. Choice H is the correct answer because it correctly states the idea that is mentioned at the end of the DNA hypothesis: that DNA amount is correlated with the amount of chromosomes.

35) In this question, we must find the answer choice that is most closely related to DNA in terms of how many characteristics it shares with the molecule. Amino acids are not found exclusively in the nucleus, so choice A is wrong. Because proteins are made of amino acids, as stated in the introductory material, they are also not found exclusively in the nucleus, so choice B is wrong. Gametes are not found in the nucleus because they are a cell with their own DNA, so choice C is wrong. Choice D is the correct answer because chromosomes are most closely related to DNA in that they are made up of DNA and they are only found in the nucleus.

36) The information necessary to answer this question is found within the introductory material before the hypotheses. However, even without knowing this specific piece of information, we have a good shot at eliminating the other incorrect answer choices.

Choice F is wrong because even a very general knowledge of the DNA hypothesis would allow you to realize that DNA is present in all cells, and not just gametes. Choice G is wrong because it is assumed in the passage that DNA is found exclusively in the nucleus. Choice H is also incorrect because DNA is not found in the nucleus and the cytoplasm. Choice J is the correct answer because it is stated in the introductory material that DNA is made of subunits called nucleotides, while proteins are made of subunits called amino acids.

37)   Look at the protein hypothesis and try to identify the main defense the author of this hypothesis has for advocating this point. This appears to be the fact that the proteins are a greater proportion of the cell than DNA, and that proteins can be made up of an infinite number of combinations of 20 amino acids. With this in mind, we can now eliminate answers. Choice B is wrong because that does not seem like a strong argument for the fact that proteins are the component of genes. It does not directly state why this would be advantageous to the theory stated in this hypothesis. Choice C is wrong because proteins are also present in the nucleus and the cytoplasm, so this argument has no credence. Choice D is incorrect because this argument actually supports the DNA hypothesis by stating that DNA levels are consistent from cell to cell with regards to the same species. Choice A is the correct answer because of the fact that all DNA is made up of combinations of 4 nucleotides as opposed to the 20 amino acids that can be used to construct proteins, which seemingly allows for more variation. This makes DNA seem less attractive compared to proteins as the material of genes.

38)   For this question, we need to see which hypothesis mentions that DNA is present only inside of the nucleus, as this is the argument that would be weakened with the information given in the question. Usually, a main point like this one would be found in the opening sentences of a hypothesis. There is no mention of DNA being exclusively contained within the nucleus in the protein hypothesis, so we can eliminate choices H and J which both contain mention that the information given in the question contradicts the protein hypothesis. Choice G is wrong because it is clear from the information given in the question that DNA is present in mitochondria, which are an organelle separate from the nucleus. Choice F is the correct answer because it is directly stated in the DNA hypothesis that DNA is found exclusively in the

nucleus. Because some genes were found in mitochondria, this contradicts the information provided in this hypothesis.

39) To answer this question we must find the central argument that that DNA hypothesis uses to prove its validity. Usually in conflicting scientist passages, this key argument is tied into why the other hypothesis(es) are incorrect. In this case, the central argument is that DNA in the same concentration in different cell types for a given organism. The central argument also states that this property is not true for proteins, Since genetic material must remain constant between all of the cells in an organism other than the gametes, this would strengthen the DNA hypothesis and greatly weaken the Protein hypothesis. Choice A is wrong because this argument would not help the DNA hypothesis and it is not mentioned in either hypothesis that the amount of protein in gametes is half the amount in other cells. Choice C is wrong because the fact that proteins are made up of combinations of smaller pieces would be supportive of a genetic role, though it may not actually have a genetic role in the cell. Choice D is wrong because it is stated in the DNA hypothesis that proteins are found outside of the nucleus, so this choice is a direct contradiction to the given information. Choice B is correct because it shows that protein content is not constant between different cells in a given organism, indicating that it is highly unlikely that genes are entirely made up of proteins.

40) For this question, we must look at information found in the introductory passage before the hypotheses are presented. In this section, it is stated that DNA is made up of subunits called nucleotides. Now we must look at the information provided in the question: AA represents amino acid, and N represents nucleotide. Since DNA is made up of nucleotide subunits, we would expect the correct answer to only have components made of N. The only answer choice that has this is choice J.

ACT WRITING (ESSAY) STRATEGY
By **Silpa Raju**

Key Essay Strategies:

-Take a clear position, but address the other side.

-Use an essay formula so that your essay will have good organization. Using a formula will not hurt your score.

-Come up with examples that clearly support your position. Go from general to specific when you introduce your examples.

-Have a few good "canned" sentences that can be customized for use in all essays. These should have good vocabulary and sentence structure.

-State the obvious and restate it.

The ACT writing test is optional, but most competitive colleges require it. The score you receive on the essay will not affect your composite score or the English score. You will get an additional Essay score (2-12) as well as a Writing score which is a combination of your English score and Essay score.

You will have 30 minutes to complete the essay, so work quickly. **If you do not write a long essay you will not get a good score**. According to the official ACT booklet, Preparing for the ACT, your essay will be graded by the following guidelines:

"Your essay will be evaluated on the evidence it gives of your ability to do the following:

- *express judgments by taking a position on the issue in writing prompt;*

- *maintain a focus on the topic throughout the essay;*
- *develop a position by using logical reasoning and by supporting your ideas;*
- *organize ideas in a logical way; and*
- *use language clearly and effectively according to the conventions of standard written English"* (Pg. 10, <u>Preparing for the ACT</u>).

What are the ACT graders told to look for in a "perfect" essay?

We quote the following from the official grading rubric:

"*Score = 6*

Essays within this score range demonstrate effective skill in responding to the task.

- *The essay shows a clear understanding of the task. The essay takes a position on the issue and may offer a critical context for discussion. The essay addresses complexity by examining different perspectives on the issue, or by evaluating the implications and/or complications of the issue, or by fully responding to counterarguments to the writer's position. Development of ideas is ample, specific, and logical. Most ideas are fully elaborated. A clear focus on the specific issue in the prompt is maintained. The organization of the essay is clear: the organization may be somewhat predictable or it may grow from the writer's purpose. Ideas are logically sequenced. Most transitions reflect the writer's logic and are usually integrated into the essay. The introduction and conclusion are effective, clear, and well developed. The essay shows a good command of language. Sentences are varied and word choice is varied and precise. There are few, if any, errors to distract the reader."* (Pg.66, <u>Preparing for the ACT</u>).

With this rubric in mind, let's go over some basic essay writing techniques. Keep in mind that not all of these will work for everyone since everyone works differently, but they're worth trying out.

Pick a side but also address the other side.

There's no "in the middle"- if you want a good score, you should pick one side. However, in order to get a high score, it is necessary to anticipate and **respond to potential counterarguments** while still focusing on one side. Pay special attention to this part of the rubric:

> "...The essay addresses complexity by examining different perspectives on the issue, or by evaluating the implications and/or complications of the issue, or by fully responding to counterarguments to the writer's position..."

This part of the rubric is unique to ACT. The rest of the rubric is similar to the SAT. Students who can get high essay scores on the SAT may not do well on the ACT essay if they are not aware of this grading requirement.

To plan or not to plan?

Preparing for the ACT recommends brainstorming before beginning to write. Our recommendation is to limit your planning to a minute and produce three examples. You can not afford to plan too long, since to get a high score you have to write a long essay. If you haven't thought of enough examples in your plan time, it would be a good idea to just begin writing and see where it takes you. If you haven't thought of all your examples by the time you're finished with your introduction paragraph, leave blanks in the sentences in your introduction to fill in later.

Five-paragraph it

A basic five paragraph essay will take you far on the ACT writing test, though it certainly isn't totally necessary. Be sure to have some sort of introduction and conclusion, and preferably three examples. However, if you can't manage to think of three examples or you prefer some other format, you can organize things differently. If you're looking for the simplest way to organize your essay, this is the way to go.

Stay on topic

The score you receive primarily is dependent on the amount of information you present to support your side, and also how effectively you present it. Therefore, your essay should be as long as you can make it while still relevant. Show an organized flow of thought with supporting examples. Try not to digress.

Introductory Paragraph

Think of a couple of generalized sentences for the introduction which you can fill in with your examples. Here's an illustration:

Happenings from _____, _____, and _____ are prime examples that support this perspective.

You should come up with your own "canned" sentence. Make sure it has some good vocabulary and sentence structure.

Don't fill in the blanks with specific examples. In the introduction use general categories, like "my personal life", "history" or "literature". Save the more specific details for later paragraphs.

You can also pre write a good "canned" sentence to use in the concluding paragraph that you can customize for the examples you happen to use for the essay. This will give your essay at least two sentences with good vocabulary and sentence structure, which should help you get a higher essay score.

A Final Note

This may seem obvious, but after each example be sure to point out exactly how it supports your position. Bluntly stating this will illustrate that you have made a clear, strong connection between the position you hold and your examples.

Similarly, in the concluding paragraph you should explicitly state why all of your examples support your position. **You do not get any extra points for being subtle. Do not hesitate to restate the obvious**.

You should now try these strategies by doing the practice essay prompt in the practice test. Then look at the sample essays scoring examples given on pages 66-71 of <u>Preparing for the ACT</u>. Pay particular attention to the essay that has the perfect score of 6 and read the explanation of the scoring. Notice how long it is and how it addresses the other side.

Notes

Notes